I0569824

MAKE IT A REALITY NOW!

How you can overcome obstacles to make your business successful in a meaningful and fulfilling way.

LEIDIS BEDOYA

MAKE IT A REALITY NOW!

Project director:

Leidis Bedoya

Editor:

Abby-Eve Editorial

Book Interior Design:

Isa Reader

Prologue:

Rev. Dr. José U. Rivera Collazo

Oikos Ministries Global

The opinions expressed in this work are solely those of the author and do not necessarily represent the opinions of any entity.

Every effort has been made to verify the accuracy of the content of this work; However, the author assumes no responsibility for errors or omissions.

For permission to reproduce copyrighted material from this publication, please contact Leidis Bedoya at the following address: 2500 W Lake Mary Blvd, office 107 F. Lake Mary, Fl. 32746.

www.leidisbedoya.com, www.hazquepaseya.com.

hello@hazquepaseya.com

This book makes it easy for readers to be responsible for creating and implementing their own decisions, physical, mental, and emotional well-being, choices, actions, and results. As such, the author is not and will not be liable for any action or inaction, or any direct or indirect result of any writing provided by the author. This book is not therapy and is not a substitute for therapy, if necessary, and it does not prevent, cure, or treat any mental, or medical disorder or disease. Workshops, manuscripts, or citations should not be used as a substitute for professional advice from law, mental conditions, doctors, or other qualified professionals and you must seek independent professional guidance for such matters.

Italics, bold and underlined areas in texts, and biblical quotations are the emphases of the author.

ISBN: 979-8-9901729-6-8 Hard Cover
ISBN: 979-8-9901729-0-6 Soft Cover Book
ISBN: 979-8-9901729-4-4 E-book
ISBN: 979-8-9901729-5-1 Audiobook
Category: Finances, Self-help techniques.

Printed in the United States of America.

The purpose of this book is to help people stimulate their inner selves, motivate the desire for action, and discover their potential in our community so that they can overcome the fear that limits them from developing a good economy, providing for their families, and creating jobs. This book aims to improve your spiritual and financial quality of life.

CONTENTS

Prologue:
Rev. Dr. José U. Rivera Collazo, Oikos Ministries Global

———————————

"MAKE IT A REALITY NOW!"

With this book, Leidis Bedoya empowers you to explore strategies. It helps to consider obstacles and possible solutions, inspire you, and give you motivation provided by first-hand knowledge and wisdom that have catapulted Leidis, respected individuals and organizations, to achieve greatness.

Faith and Belief are two terms more frequently associated with theology than commerce.

However, these two concepts become the first and most important pillars of any business initiative event.

Many can write about theoretical ideology associated with a culminating statement about defining success but failing to provide practical experience from a thought to its realization.

There are no shortcuts to success. However, you can use great and wise advice from Leidis Bedoya whose faith and belief are rooted in the earth and whose motivation symbolizes extending your branches with her experience related to business. Through this book, you will be reaching to the heavens in search of inspiration and guidance.

I have known Leidis for a decade as a close friend, spiritual daughter, mother, motivational speaker, and successful businesswoman. She speaks from her heart, experiences, determination, and collaboration within the community. You will be inspired by this dynamic and entertaining narrative, as you navigate and explore your business venture. I am confident that this book will help point your compass in the path to success and experience great motivation after reading it.

Rev. Dr. José U. Rivera Collazo
Oikos Ministries Global

Introduction
I Made It Happen

My country, Colombia, is a wonderful land full of treasures and natural landscapes. A place that, over the years, has grown and evolved significantly, becoming a benchmark in Latin America. However, in my childhood and adolescence, in certain areas, people lived in an environment full of fear and uncertainty.

I was born and raised in a very humble neighborhood in the city of Medellín. At a young age, it was normal to hear about bombs in the center of the city and violence near the places where family and friends were, and that is why many scenes are recorded in my memory where I see myself praying and crying that nothing would happen to my father. My mother, for her part, did not let me leave my house beyond what was strictly necessary out of fear (something I understood in my adulthood), so from my small confinement, my mind allowed me to travel, enjoy, and create only in my mind. I couldn't go out and play with my friends like other children I saw through the window because doing so was putting myself at risk—from my mother's point of view.

In Medellín, there are very stable, beautiful, and high-income neighborhoods, but where I lived at that time, what I saw in most of the people around me was scarcity. People lived by borrowing money, getting items from the store to pay later, and being in great need. It was normal to go out and see young people taking drugs on the corners, spending hours and hours sitting in a group, talking, without any notable job, as if they just wanted to wait for time to pass. I didn't know them or how they spent their time, but that was all I saw when I went from my house to school. I noticed that it was sadly common to see people involved in drugs, killings, or gangs as if that were the only alternative. I perceived conformity in people's actions and did not understand why they complained so much instead of looking for solutions. I even noticed in some people a resentment toward anyone who did well, even if they did well by doing things differently, while they were failing unintentionally without options, and some of them did nothing to change their circumstances.

But none of that limited my ability to dream or long for a better future for myself, my family, and those who found it impossible to get out of the cycle of scarcity and limitations. So, I decided to change my life and my finances without waiting for perfect circumstances or for someone else to do it for me.

I worked hard for it, living the experiences for myself and checking that what I recommend works by trying it myself first before wanting to help others.

Every healthy, crazy thing I wanted to do, I tried and achieved, producing benefits for many. I verified that it was possible, even today, to move forward, despite any circumstance, no matter how difficult it may be; assuming the moments of greatest difficulty with positivity and enthusiasm is one of my keys.

As a result of all that effort, I was able to finish my studies, paying for them myself, something that was unthinkable a long time ago. I began to invest a lot of time preparing to help others, to enjoy and be grateful for all the blessings I began to receive, activating the faith that helped me not fall into difficult times.

Without wanting to and without looking for it, I have learned to fall and get up quickly and with a good attitude; I have healed a lot of what hurt, and I have understood that without God, I am nothing. I have used what I know to become someone who manages their businesses and promotes the businesses of others, someone who creates and develops projects that are difficult to achieve, a woman of faith who goes on missions, visits low-income neighborhoods to give lectures on how to get ahead and start a business, and who also enjoys financial freedom that I would never have imagined enjoying. Truly living with purpose is priceless.

So, what do I do with all that experience? The best thing anyone can do is *share* it. The commitment and weight of my conscience are too great to keep such a great treasure for myself. So why not help these valuable secrets spread around the world? Why not allow others to do so?

That is why you have this book in your hands today because I want to help you, practically and concretely, to believe that if all of this was possible for me and for many entrepreneurs whom I have been able to help on this path, it could also be possible for you.

In this book, you will find the steps you need to follow to:

- Live from your business.

- Be prepared if, at any time, your current survival plan doesn't work.

- Change your route if you get tired or feel like you haven't achieved any of your dreams.

- Improve what you have now.

- If you already have everything you want, feel fulfilled with your dreams, and already use all your talents, this book will also help you reaffirm what works among successful people.

Everything in it has been tested and supported throughout my more than twenty years of professional experience. You will also find real evidence and testimonies of people who have also achieved success (we have changed the names of some of them to preserve their identity), which will serve as inspiration so that, starting today, you can work on the personal, spiritual, emotional, and financial success that your life needs.

My main motivation has been the immense gratitude for having overcome so many obstacles in which it is normal to feel defeated and not stop anymore; moments that come into the life of any person where we have no control over what happens to us, but we do have control of how to get out, take action and change our mentality for our benefit. I think that, **yes, you can** get ahead, and, **yes, you can** materialize all your projects during difficulties. You deserve to be happy and enjoy everything that life brings you, the good and the bad, in a positive way if you overcome your fears and work on your weaknesses.

My greatest wish is to hear from you, as I have heard from many other brave people, that your story can become a success story. I wish for you to achieve the life you want so that with fruits and authority, we can help others achieve it.

Don't let time pass. MAKE IT A REALITY... NOW!

Part One:
You Have the Keys!

Chapter
ONE
IN SEARCH OF A PURPOSE

When we have a meaning, a reason to live, and a motivation, a feeling of importance is created in our subconscious. It is something that happens within each person and that others often do not understand. It is as if we were created especially for a mission in life that prevents us from having so many voids. This purpose helps us understand that we were designed with love, unique talents, and virtues, that sometimes we do not recognize our value, and that it is required to be worth occupying space in this life. Purpose drives us when the people we love do not support us, when we feel rejection or abandonment from others, and even when we abandon ourselves. It is the answer to why we are here and why we feel like this.

When there is no good purpose to fight for, emptiness and loneliness remain, and paths become confused. It is then when, sometimes, we realize the hard way that the dreams of others have been fulfilled, but what about our own? Where did they end up? Did they temporarily fade away? How important is your life? Everything, absolutely everything, has consequences, and what we do about it ourselves will help us get ahead when we need it.

Living with purpose makes us wake up with an inner happiness that leads us to know ourselves better and to do what we were born to do. It allows us to enjoy and take on challenges with the certainty that we can achieve them because there is a beyond, a reason why we are the way we are. When we understand it, each job we do has much more importance because we are aware of the effect we produce. After all, even a smile or a word can change someone's life.

We are all good at something different, which is wonderful because it makes us need each other more and appreciate what others can do. We have a purpose for being born into the family we were born into, being part of the new family we have, belonging to our circle of friends, and a great purpose with the people we meet in life.

In my case, my purpose has been determined by a high gratitude to God for all the blessings He has given me in a way that exceeds all human possibilities. The miracles that occurred in someone as normal as me, even during pain, awakened in me the deep desire to share what has worked for me.

I understand that there is a purpose behind the fact that in so many areas of my life, I am going the way I am, and if I didn't value that, I wouldn't be so sure that what happened to me, good and bad, was worth it.

Having a purpose helped me live for something bigger than problems, demotivation, loneliness, and past disappointments. It helped me to have the certainty of knowing that walking behind Him, helps improve the quality of life of many people, encouraging many to overcome their financial crises and regain their peace. Wanting to help has given me purpose, experience, knowledge, and guidance. This life is temporary; sometimes, our fears and emotions don't let us see further until we know what we were born for.

When you live with purpose and there are results, the right people come. You feel motivated when you see your dreams and those of many people come true.

A good purpose, whatever it may be if it is discovered, reveals a great reason to continue in this life and is the main and most excellent motivator to undertake it successfully.

How can we discover what can help ourselves and others? We must ask ourselves: 'What potential do we see in ourselves, with our work or our daily lives, that can contribute to helping the community live with purpose?'

We need to believe that it is possible to have a purpose with dreams, to be happy doing what we like, using our talents and the gifts that God gave us as part of that mission. We all have something special, something that is rare, that is unique, talents that we do not even use, and often, we do not give them the importance they have.

Talent is the deep light, your guide, your inner grain of sand that helps you determine how you can be happier and how you can live your day-to-day life. Have you realized that sometimes (and this is a mistake), we do not give value to what we are given, and we only take care of what we have paid or fought for? Well, many times, that happens with our talents.

I discovered my talent in business, and now I feel the commitment to leave a legacy with what I have lived, practiced, and acquired because I firmly believe that I will be able to help many people through my purpose. This is a very interesting topic because finances are crucial in any life since bad decisions can considerably affect the lives of many families and those close to them. Therefore, if we organize our administrative areas, we can have a purpose beyond making our homes or lives more fruitful.

A Story of Power

I want to share with you the story of someone who found his purpose and his why at forty-seven years old. His name is José, and he is the founder and CEO of two successful companies in the area of vacation properties and renovations for an investment company.

José had been repairing and renovating houses for many years. He felt so much passion for it; he did it so well, and it gave him so much satisfaction to see the joy in the people to whom he had provided his services throughout his life that, without a doubt, he understood that this was his purpose. In addition to this, at his age, he wanted to feel that he could work in something that would allow him to enjoy a better quality of life, be on his schedule, and spend more time with his family.

In the beginning, his main fear was becoming independent and failing, especially because he had been working in his last job for another company for more than ten years, working stably as an engineer at ISP. However, his purpose drove him to make decisions overcoming difficulties.

One of them was when he decided to start the vacation rental business and he was having a hard time finding clients. Not having a traditional rental model and not having enough time to get reviews or make the business known was a difficult task for him. But José set out to work in marketing areas, learned how to manage the system to attract more people, improved his properties, and quickly matched his previous salary with the freedom and purpose he wanted to achieve. He could work through his challenges to achieve his goals and overcome his obstacles, and he began renting his vacation spots using multiple platforms.

José today has more time to be with his family and enjoy his children, which is what he feels has the most value in his life. Being able to have long vacations with them and be happy with the people he loves is priceless for him. Furthermore, as he owns his own business, he can organize his schedules or delegate to his team, always meeting his client's needs with excellence, and at the same time, he can dedicate himself to other projects that give him pleasure while still fulfilling all his responsibilities. He does not feel any regrets, as he is proud of everything he has achieved in such a short time.

This businessman affirms that the greatest advantage he had in being able to start, added to his talents and qualities, was his faith in God and the conviction that if he had a good purpose, everything would be fine. He identified his great purpose, talents, and qualities to decide on which business was unique for him, and in the face of each challenge, he prepared to do it well and gain experiences in the future. All this without leaving aside the fact that he is a strong and persevering worker and an innately brave man who is not afraid of any type of project, and if he feels afraid, he still takes the step, and things turn out well for him. He also has an advantage that allows him to please his clients with a very good attitude to solve any problem because he is a naturally calm and patient person with the characteristic of not letting opportunities slip away.

Jose feels convinced that having your own business is a good idea because he has proven that it is possible to have a better quality of life for himself and his family. He used his passion, moved to action, and activated his faith, obtaining effective results.

His advice for someone who doesn't have a job right now or wants to pursue a dream is: "First, have faith in God. Second, start with something you like and are good at. Third, dedicate time to your business, especially when you are starting. Fourth, use all free tools, such as the internet and social media, to promote your business or sell your product. And fifth, follow these tips. With discipline and dedication, you will achieve it."

The purpose goes hand in hand with a good plan and a marketing study in the area you chose, designed just for you, and having that purpose included as a priority. This step is important to start your project with responsibility and diligence.

Take your time to find your purpose, and once you find it, it will be the fire that ignites your engine.

Proverbs 21:5, NLT

"Good planning and hard work lead to prosperity, but hasty shortcuts lead to poverty."

Reflect:

- What do you think you are in this life for?

_____

_____

- Do you think that in your work, with your family, or in your businesses, you are working with purpose?

_____

_____

- What potential do you see in yourself to contribute to the community and live with purpose?

_____

_____

- Do you have the full desire to fulfill a purpose, whatever your daily routine is? What is the real purpose of why you want to start your business?

_____

_____

- Would you be happier if you used your natural or acquired talents to live with purpose?

_____

_____

Take a minute to stop and think about the temporality of this life and what your legacy in it may be.

Chapter TWO

DISCOVER AND BELIEVE IN YOUR POTENTIAL AND TALENTS

Discovering your potential is one of the best gifts you can give yourself on the fascinating journey of life. It is what allows you to enjoy success and the satisfaction of knowing that you have something special that others do not have.

The potential is like a chest with many keys, and each of them can open or close doors to unlimited opportunities. A chest full of treasure, which is permanently pricked by spears that you must dodge to find what is inside for you. Some of them are the criticisms that take away your motivation and the fears and insecurities that prevent you from achieving what is yours.

By diving into the depth of your being and who you are and exploring both the positive and what holds you back, you will be able to find in every corner of that chest your skills, knowledge, and passions, and by discovering your purpose, you will be able to bring out your full potential and use it for your benefit first, and then that of others. This inner journey invites you to recognize and value the jewels you already own and to create new ones that go hand in hand with them, preparing you and becoming an expert with the experience that only time gives.

> *We often find a treasure hidden deep within our being, and with insecurities, we deny our inner capacity. But I want you to read this: even if you don't give yourself the right value, your potential is there, and you have to discover it.*

Discovering your potential is being sure of what you know how to do well and letting others see it. But how can you make others know you if you haven't even discovered yourself?

Seek your potential and hold on to it no matter who you have around you. Hold on to what no one can take away from you. Discover what you are very good at because that is like an arsenal of tools that unlock the path to your entrepreneurship. You may lose some people or material things, but no one can take from you your talents, what you know, and your potential. You are the only one responsible for not losing it, for not letting die what is in your heart waiting for you to open paths to the life you want. The key is to fight that little enemy in your mind that makes you doubt.

What you know how to do, not everyone can achieve; what you know, not everyone knows; what you have, many people desperately want and need.

But it's not just about knowing that you have potential; it's about using it and improving it with humility every day so that it doesn't fade away. It's knowing that every day, you have something different to learn and that all of this helps you get new keys in the chest that unlock success in your business endeavors.

A treasure has no value if no one gives it to you; if it is hidden, that is why you need to discover yourself. This will make you a confident person, present a product without fear, and make you certain that what you have is valuable. That will be motivation and a shield for when someone tells you that your dreams are worthless, that you don't have the ability, but if you believe it, you will listen to what they tell you, and you will be able to understand and respect without agreeing and without being paralyzed. If you know what you have, that's power!

A Story of Power

This is an example of a successful entrepreneur who found his potential:

Joel is the founder and CEO of Avofuel, a successful restaurant located in Florida. Being a medical professional was a promising career that many desired, and after only practicing for about a year, he realized that this was not what he was passionate about. So how could Joel be more fruitful and happier?

He decided to start a business, following the legacy of his parents, who had a restaurant in Puerto Rico, and applying his **passion**, which encompasses health, good nutrition, and training. With all these elements, he founded a restaurant with a different concept, having avocado as the main ingredient in all his organic and healthy dishes. He knew that using his talents and advancing as a tireless worker, virtues inherited from his parents, was very important, and that is why he decided to set goals and new challenges no matter how difficult they might be.

His biggest fear initially was starting in such a saturated field, without any type of experience or training, and that the public would not accept the concept. But despite his fears, he sought and worked with the potential he discovered in himself and made the decision to follow a path based on his passion. This involved, among other things, acquiring basic culinary knowledge before creating her dishes and recipes and ensuring that the texture of her flavor profile was well-balanced. He used his passion for motivating and preparing himself with his talents, as well as in other areas such as accounting, operations, product costs, and marketing while researching, planning, and designing each idea in his restaurant. After so much uncertainty, dedication, and a vision made a reality, today you can see the fruits.

The most difficult moment for him, but at the same time, it was the most blessing, was when the pandemic arrived. At that time, by government mandate, many restaurants closed, but he—at that time operating from a small food *truck*[1]—decided to continue opening to the public. Seeing the positive in a negative situation where many gave up, he admirably continued to fight with positivity. He was even part of a small documentary made by an important news network, highlighting how a fighting warrior handled himself in moments of crisis, and from there, he was able to motivate others to continue. What seemed like an obstacle became an opportunity that marked a key moment in his growth through enthusiasm, confidence, and, most significantly, hard work.

Joel is sure that the great advantage of having his own business is being able to be himself, with the freedom to decide and set the direction of his company. He states that he has never regretted the change from medicine to entrepreneurship since, from an early age, he had the strength to make the biggest decision of his life, and that was that "when he had to choose, he would choose his happiness." He discovered his true potential and chose not to pursue a career in which he felt he didn't fit, and almost twenty years later, he is at peace and content because that decision turned out to be a blessing. The admirable thing about Joel in achieving his goals as a

---

[1]   Food truck or restaurant on wheels.

successful entrepreneur was that he always knew that obstacles were a product of his mind, and he never saw anything that prevented him from working toward his goals.

As a result, Joel is now earning the same as he would in a career that for many would be difficult to exceed, but he did it, working for himself, without pressure, and without having to follow some structure or protocol defined by someone else. Today, he is enjoying all the benefits because he has dared to continue ignoring his initial fears.

Joel has a strong mindset that we are in this world to fulfill a purpose. Each of us is capable of dreaming big and fighting for what belongs to us. "It all starts with a small idea and trusting yourself," he says.

"Having your own business," shares Joel, "means having a purpose, being completely happy, doing what you dream of, and at the same time discovering along the way the true potential and skills that one had not yet discovered. Having your own business is being able to materialize a vision in your mind out of nothing and, after so many years of sacrifice, being able to look from the outside and say, 'I did it!'"

Today, Joel shares his story to help others see their potential and thanks all the people who contributed from the beginning and took their time to help him because not only did he see his potential, but all of those who supported him saw it, too. He also thanked all the customers who have made Avofuel a successful company.

If we could see the natural talents that God gave us and appreciate what we know how to do as a treasure and give value to that, we could advance further and feel happier with what we do. In the story I just told you, Joel was diligent and prepared, took action, used his potential, and achieved it.

I enjoy seeing people's businesses succeed so that they know that it is possible despite the obstacles that life brings. I motivate them because it gives me satisfaction. And what gives you satisfaction?

"**Proverbs 22:1-3, NIV**

"1. A good name is more desirable than great riches;
to be esteemed is better than silver or gold.

2. Rich and poor have this in common: The LORD is the Maker
of them all.

3. The prudent see danger and take refuge, but the simple keep
going and pay the penalty".

---

1 Corinthians 12:7, NLT

"A spiritual gift is given to each of
us so we can help each other".

Reflect

- What activity do you enjoy so much that you could do it every day? How would you feel if you earned money for that?

  _____

  _____

- Do you think you are good at creating projects?

  _____

  _____

- What are your natural talents, and what are your learned talents?

  _____

  _____

- What do you do well, and what can you improve?

  _____

  _____

- What are the weaknesses that prevent you from finding your potential?

  _____

  _____

- Do you believe in yourself? Do you have to work on it?

  _____

  _____

To achieve success, you must analyze yourself in detail, know yourself, and take the time to feel if these answers motivate you, scare you, or if you ignore them. If you do not give the necessary importance to discovering yourself, you will waste a lot of time in your life, and it may be that after time passes, you will find yourself frustrated doing something that does not give you happiness or that you do not want to continue doing.

Chapter
THREE

FIND WHAT MOTIVATES YOU

Unless you are one of the lucky few who benefited from an inheritance, family or external support, won the lottery, or some other exceptional blessing, you need to get to work because whether you like it or not, we are in a world where you have to work to survive. Therefore, once you find your purpose, discover your potential, and are ready to work on the basic keys to success, you need to motivate yourself to start.

But how do you find what motivates you to start your engines and take the course of your long-awaited path, overcoming the obstacles that life brings?

Many find it by supporting their children, parents, other family members, partners, or someone else who becomes their motivation to fight. Usually, it is a person they want to help, someone they admire, or someone they love.

Some others found their motivating force in their highest power, chosen according to personal spiritual beliefs, with what they learned from lived experiences or family traditions.

There are also cases of people who have gone through difficult times, and after getting tired of the world failing them, they discover that if they have God, they have everything. Then, they feel saved and motivated because they understand that they are not alone and that they are chosen and loved wonderfully. They find their motivation in working every day with deep gratitude to God for all the blessings, and that is why they decide to live with purpose. In my case, that is my reason. I recognize that my faith and gratitude, added to the immense desire to help, is what has served as my motivation and success in my businesses. Although sometimes it sounds incredible to others, knowing that we work for Him, for God, for Jesus, is a unique motivator.

I know many people have something or someone different to believe in that motivates them. I have to be realistic: we all have the right to believe in what we want and live the life we prefer. That greater outer power is a great help in trusting that everything will be okay no matter what happens, but I share what I feel and what has worked for me: my faith. A faith that I have seen bears fruit since I was very little because very strange things have happened to me, and I have always turned out well. I don't know why since many situations have been very hard to overcome, and sometimes, it hasn't made sense for me to feel so protected.

Motivation is something that must be constantly worked on since it is not always with us. Sometimes, it is due to health situations, external circumstances, or not taking care of what is around us or those close to us. We are human, vulnerable, and have weaknesses, and it is okay to accept that it is often difficult to stay motivated.

Something that affects motivation and brings enormous problems is not knowing who we listen to or what we put in front of our eyes and ears, as well as not correctly choosing to whom and how we talk about our things. If someone to whom you present your projects is not ready to listen, or it is not the right time to tell them, you will probably have a negative response that will begin to make you lose that motivation you worked so hard for.

Matthew 7:15-20, KJV

"Beware of false prophets, which come to you in sheep's clothing, but inwardly they are ravening wolves. Ye shall know them by their fruits. Do men gather grapes of thorns, or figs of thistles? Even so every good tree bringeth forth good fruit; but a corrupt tree bringeth forth evil fruit. A good tree cannot bring forth evil fruit, neither can a corrupt tree bring forth good fruit. Every tree that bringeth not forth good fruit is hewn down, and cast into the fire. Wherefore by their fruits ye shall know them."

What heart does the person who wants to help you have? Do you feel happy that someone else is doing well? Are you jealous of others? Do they have the ability, and have you seen them destroy others?

Sometimes you know that you have the secret for someone to do well and you have the desire to help them, or you feel the need to express your dreams and you don't analyze who you vent to, and in the end, you end up neglecting your thoughts and your heart, which is something very valuable. Please remember: when it's not time, it's not time. Learning from other people's experiences helps us not to fall so many times, but ego, pessimism, tragedy, and stubbornness distract us and make us deaf when it comes to listening when it is time to learn. If this were not the case, how much advice would we have heard from our parents who, with love, guided us?

Not all advice is good, but listening to wise advice, which comes from love, knowledge, and experience, can help you grow and develop as a person and as a businessperson. Take a moment to think: where and with whom do you spend your energy?

Matthew 7:6 (NIV)

"Do not give dogs what is sacred; do not throw your pearls to pigs. If you do, they may trample them under their feet, and turn and tear you to pieces."

Staying motivated is vital to moving your business forward amidst obstacles. Analyze who you are going to follow and who you are going to listen to. It is very important to reflect on where you focus, what you dedicate time to, what your mind receives, and who the people are around you. If, even unconsciously, you are causing your family to receive negativity from you, you will be sowing thoughts in them that will affect their attitudes.

In my case, it works for me to ask: "Lord, give me wisdom to speak, to think, to act." He listens to you; ask, and it will be given to you. This process for me is strong because I see situations and feel confident that there is a better path, salvation, and a faster and safer way for your business to do well.

Mattew 7:7-8, NIV

"Ask and it will be given to you; seek and you will find; knock and the door will be opened to you. For everyone who asks receives; the one who seeks finds; and to the one who knocks, the door will be opened."

Having faith is essential for progress. In my experience, I have seen how faith and the discernment of having it allows you to identify whether the person is ready to listen to you or not. I have learned to understand that, and if the person listening to me is not asking me for help or wanting it, I prefer to respect their opinion and wait for the appropriate moment in which God will use me to transmit his message when the person is willing to listen, willing to grow.

We are human, and we have emotions; we have the right not to feel good when our body or our mind takes us to that state, but for our good, it is very important to have the ability to ask for help and learn every day from others. Finding ways to motivate ourselves is our responsibility if we want to get ahead. In my case, I like to learn every day from others and learn from the problems and situations that we all go through; I like to grow by reading and watching motivational videos, and I also like people who know how to seek help. I admire those who do not let themselves be carried away by their feelings and always try to find a way to move forward. After all, by asking for help, we have nothing to lose.

For me, life is a journey full of satisfaction that I live exploring my talents, taking risks with what I like, and living healthy adventures, including writing this book, a dream that I could materialize thanks to the fruits that other companies I manage gave me. How can I not believe that having your business is a good idea if it has been a great blessing for me and others? It is a pleasure to generate projects, and it is a pleasure when someone or an employee tells you, "I can study, I can invest, I can progress because of the opportunity that your business provides."

I like to see how people progress, and it saddens me to see doors close to someone who can't get a job or that they or their families suffer for money. That's why I put all my effort into ensuring that people can use all these tools so that they don't have to depend on anyone to progress, even if they don't have resources, even if they have to start only with services provided to others, even if they don't have the money to buy products now. If they can only start from the bottom and grow slowly, I want to help them advance by understanding that a little is better than nothing because that little can become a lot.

I want to tell you that one day, you will laugh remembering when you didn't get a job anywhere or what you found wasn't what you wanted, and you will remember the moment when only your personality as an unstoppable entrepreneur led your small business to grow and grow and grow until you enjoy what you have. The formula is simple, but sometimes it is not followed due to stubbornness, fear, or ego, for making bad decisions, for not seeking justice for the client or oneself, or for not providing a good product, which is essential. Being able to sleep peacefully and feel pride in the things that were done well is phenomenal and priceless. . You are motivated by the fact that you enjoy your progress with the appropriate values and know that things are done well.

The Keys are in Your Hands

In these first three chapters, we have established the foundations to form a business, which is done by finding your purpose, discovering your potential, and your motivation. All of this essential knowledge that I have shared with you is based on my own experiences and is common among successful people.

I know starting or continuing sometimes is not easy, but something that can help you is to think about your home, your life, your business, what worries you, and what brings conflict in your organization. Without judging or blaming others, think: what can you do to find solutions? What can you contribute to overcome your weaknesses and those of others, based on the keys presented above? What are you good at, and with those talents, how can you grow with your organization?

We are not perfect, and as humans, we have many flaws, but for a better life and success in business, we must assume what we should work on and do it with humility. The fruits and the positive come on the way as a gift that compensates the efforts. So, why not live in harmony? Why not be the best we can be? Help your loved ones to be the best they can be, to climb as high as they can, like eagles. If your people are well, you will be better. A mistake made by many people who find it difficult to progress is not valuing or not helping those who are by their side but, on the contrary, overshadowing them. If your partner or your workers do something well, are happy, and progress together as a team, they will get ahead more easily. Are you not helping your loved ones because of insecurity or fear of losing them?

In my case, I understand that everything I have in this life is borrowed and that if I don't manage it well, I will lose it. If what I do has no purpose beyond it, my efforts are not worth it. I enjoy it, and I enjoy it if my family is as well. If my friends prosper, it gives me satisfaction. At the end of the day, we are here temporarily. In this way, I feel that there is peace and satisfaction that no money can buy because material wealth becomes stronger when it goes together with spiritual wealth.

Many successful entrepreneurs claim that the people you surround yourself with have a large influence on your success or failure. So, what if you build with the people around you a relationship of high respect, health, and harmony, without sought conflicts, without violence, without envy, without being afraid that they are well, due to your insecurities? What if we ensure that no one feels bad because someone else is doing well, because they fulfill their dreams, without thinking that people who make money are always bad or don't deserve it?

If you think that people doing well are doing wrong, be careful with your words and consider whether those words edify or demotivate those who trust you with their dreams. If you believe that someone who is doing well does not deserve anything more, you are limiting your potential too, because you will feel guilty if you do well, and it is not fair to you because you also have your value. What you are is yours to use as you wish.

You have the right to be prosperous, to be happy, and to enjoy what you have worked for, whether for yourself or to help others. If, in your business or your personal life, your words are destroyed with negativity, it will be more difficult to create good relationships, have people of human quality nearby, and keep clients for a long time since life brings its difficulties, its obstacles, and when people seek to feel positive, they easily distance themselves from those who make them feel bad.

I invite you to be someone who attracts good things and gives good things.

Analyze your words, your tone of voice, and the message you convey when you express yourself. This will cause you to have better relationships, more success, live with purpose, and discover your value for your clients, your family, and your friends.

Do not feel envious of the success of others; use this feeling to grow, find your mission, and have the courage to fulfill your desires, regardless of the past, age, or what you can no longer change. What's done is done, but you have the opportunity right now to heal and contribute to others' healing and to be a person of light for others.

Do not overshadow anyone's dreams, and do not play with the sensitivity of others as a joke. We do not know what is in each world or what that person is trying to heal.

If you repeat discouraging expressions to others, they stay in your thoughts and your subconscious, only affecting you and negatively advising yourself. Encourage others! By encouraging others, you are also encouraging yourself.

REFLECT:

After analyzing and responding in the reflection spaces at the end of each chapter, I want to invite you to answer these questions before continuing.

- Do you fulfill your life purpose?

- Are you using your full potential with your found value?

- What is your value?

- What aspects of your personality contribute to your circle (family, friendships, or business)?

- How can you combine your purpose, your potential, and the remaining keys to achieve your goal?

- With your words and your attitude, are you being light or dark for others?

Part Two:
In Search of the Doors

Chapter FOUR

THE KEY PIECES OF A BUSINESS

When you buy something that comes disassembled, you need to pay attention and not leave any parts loose because otherwise, when you put it together, it won't work. It's the same with a business: if you want it to work, you need to have all the essential pieces to move it forward. In this way, you will reap all those desired fruits that will take you to the path of what you have defined as success. Remember that we all call success differently, but whatever your ideal is, all these pieces are essential so that the structure does not fall.

There are determining factors for the success of a business, depending on the industry in which a person decides to focus, and there are others that apply to any endeavor or business sector. Some of the determining factors are good administration, good attitude, positivity, faith, good marketing, perseverance, responsibility, and an immense desire to improve. All of this is followed by action and the assurance that it will be achieved.

Below, I present some fundamental principles that are essential for most businesses. These are the key pieces for your business success:

- **Find your purpose**.

- **Discover your value in your potential**. Clearly define what makes you different from the competition and what unique value you offer your customers.

- **Find your point of faith**, what people call "your highest power"; that which you believe and trust in, that gives you conviction and protects you. It's what leads you to believe that miracles exist and that you will be fine.

- **Use your purpose and your value to find your talents and your type of business only** based on your being, not on what others do.

- **Plan responsibly**. Educate yourself, research, plan, and inform yourself about the appropriate requirements, as well as budget costs and profits. Rationally, seek to make sense of the business with deep analysis on your part. Develop a clear and well-structured business plan that includes your objectives, vision, mission, and realistic strategies with a market analysis.

- ***Find a product that helps your clients.*** *If the product you sell only benefits you as the owner, you will be one of the few people who buy from you.* Customers more easily buy a product that they consider benefits them, which is why sales presentations seek to create a need and then satisfy it with the product or service that is offered. Many businesses fail because contracts represent problems for customers instead of benefits. Furthermore, if what you offer helps your clients, you will be motivated to do it with a purpose beyond money; therefore, it will come by itself. This will allow you to adapt your offer and marketing strategies more effectively. Customer satisfaction is key to long-term success, including offering high-quality products or services with a customer focus.

- **Make use of marketing with results.** You can have a treasure, but no one will find it if it is hidden. So, if you have your product, you must make it known! How to do it? Developing firm and proven marketing strategies. To do this, you must think about your audience: what type of marketing would be effective for people in the age range you want to reach? What area do you live in? What are your preferences? You can initially use all the free digital-focused platforms, in addition to other traditional options, but if you have the possibility, the best thing you can do is rely on an expert.

Good marketing improves your product, and making it known is essential. So that you don't lose money, analyze your product carefully and what is the wisest way to invest your resources. What can you do, and what do you need to delegate? Marketing is very important to overcome the obstacle of how to get customers.

- **Develop good financial management**. A successful business has profits and not losses, and if at some point they occur, then there is something to improve. Maintain strict financial control, maintain a budget, constantly track income and expenses, and plan for the future.

Many businesses generate enough income and still do not prosper. If the failure is in how you are managing, you have to make extreme decisions to save your business. The person in charge of managing a business must have the strength and character to save, the ability to maintain reserves, to say "no" if it is not necessary to buy something or the business cannot cover it at the moment, know how much comes in and how much can be spent. You must enjoy the order of documents, sales, and purchase records.

If you, as the owner, do not feel capable, or the person in charge does not like the responsibilities or does not carry out these tasks correctly, you must find the missing piece. Assigning someone qualified and willing to do the job, who has these characteristics innately, will be a good idea.

Administration is the basis for sustaining the success of a company and even the success of your home's finances.

If you don't manage or delegate well, it will be like a broken bag where, just as the money comes in, it goes out, and the worst thing is that you realize it when you are already lost. This is not only for businesses: poor administration also affects many families. Some people or businesses earn much less but manage very well, so they fulfill all their wishes. Most importantly, they have peace knowing that they have stability and that they are not going to lose what they have worked for.

We are not perfect, and sometimes we learn this the hard way. Some people do not experiment with someone else's mind and have to change and start again with a different mentality. If that is your fault, fire the administrator and get a new person in that area. Save your business or your family so you can prosper as you deserve. Seek professional help, talk to your accountant, and educate yourself in all the areas you feel unprepared for.

- **Pick a good team.** If you have the opportunity, choose people who are better than you, but if they are not and they have the right attitude, they learn efficiently, if they are people who listen, who follow instructions, and are good at solving any obstacle with you, it is worth investing your time in them. Personality and attitude are basic qualities. This helps fulfill your internal operations.

If your company is efficient, this contributes to productivity, saves resources, and helps you have satisfied customers.

- **Adapt to the changes.** Being open to innovation and change helps you adapt and grow your business. Being flexible and improving according to market changes keeps you abreast of trends and technologies that, in the end, can be innovative for your business or even your personal life.

- **Appreciate your work team**. Promotes a positive work environment and stable company culture. You are the one who manages your venture, the fundamental piece, but your team is the heart of your company. When you delegate, your company is in their hands, and thanks to them, you grow. Without help, it is more difficult to grow. You and your team need each other: you have the bravery and responsibilities they don't want, and they provide you with the services for which they are compensated. In the end, if everyone works as a team, everyone goes further. They are as important as you. Understanding this will help you improve employee retention and productivity.

- **Keep your promises with product quality and humanity**. The worst thing is to be begging a company to deliver a service or product as they promised. If you can't deliver something you promise, don't do it. Explain the realistic times in which you can accomplish this so as not to frustrate any customers. Remember: you are here to help with your product. On many occasions, **the customer does not remember the product, but they do remember the experience**. This helps you gain referrals effectively and have repeat customers.

- **Put the customer at the center of your business decisions**. What do they want? What do you like? Listen to their feedback and adapt your offer accordingly. Develops the ability to listen and enjoy giving what someone needs, not what you want to give.

Remember that these are general guidelines, and each business may require specific approaches. The ability to learn, adapt, and make continuous and successful changes that lead to prosperity are also keys to business success.

Many business ideas are excellent, but they have not managed to grow due to a lack of organization, guidance, waste, and poor financial decisions. May this not be your case.

— Proverbs 28:25, NAS

"An arrogant man stirs up strife, but he who trusts in the LORD will prosper."

> ## — Psalms 92:14, NKJV
>
> *"They shall still bear fruit in old age;*
> *They shall be fresh and flourishing."*

Reflect

- Are you complying with all these principles?

- Which one do you need to work on?

- Why do you think you don't comply?

- What are the necessary expenses of your business, and which are not?

- Are you willing to make an effort not to spend on what is not necessary until the business is generating enough income to do so without harming you?

- When can you start working on what you need?

- Do you think this is important? Why?

Chapter FIVE

WHERE TO START?

You already have your purpose, you have found your value and your motivation, you follow all the steps to get the keys, and you have all the faith possible... And now what? Well, now comes the action because without action, we are nothing. Some people lack much of the above and make great progress just because they take action. So, how do you go from one side to the other? Well, the most important thing you can do is **BEGIN**, move, and remove the "but, but, but" that hold you back and mental obstacles to get what you want until you get it.

Remember: nothing will ever be perfect, so if you wait until you have everything to start fulfilling your dreams, the road will be more difficult, and it will take longer to start growing.

> *If you have all the resources to start, start; if not, start anyway.*

Everything you already planned, do it! You can start by creating the name of your company, registering it, looking for your identification number, hiring, or filling out all the forms you need yourself to be up to date with all the requirements. If you don't know, look for a professional, pick up the phone, and make the necessary calls to get everything you need to open and maintain your business, set dates, and start doing your work with organization, enthusiasm, and dedication. The action must be aimed at providing a service that you want to receive. But MAKE IT A REALITY... NOW!

Healthy opportunities for progress often come and go, and we don't know if we will see them again. You have to take advantage of that desire, that spark of life, and go ahead and do it. The **ACTION** It is essential for fulfillment. Prepare, plan, look for solutions for each outcome in the worst and best situations, and write them down so that you feel more prepared and comfortable to start without the fear of not knowing how to solve any situation in advance. Nothing is lost by trying.

Planning, investigating, carrying out, and taking the reins with action will come from the inner desire, from the passion you feel when using your talents because you know that you do it well or because you have the motivation to seek to be the best. Don't let those dreams and desires go out and start. Go after that feeling that tells you: "Just do it and go for it."

The decision of whether you want to work for someone else or start your business is very personal. Both are very good and respectable, but in this book, you will see that my focus is to encourage and guide people who want to make a living from their own business, using their talents, their virtues, and their faith to get ahead. Working for someone else gives you stability since the risk is assumed by someone else (in many cases, the profits for a business are also greater), while undertaking the risk is much higher, you have more responsibilities in your charge, but it is worth it. I know this is scary, but when you like what you do, and it makes you happy, you will notice that those responsibilities are easier to carry.

Having a business is an adventure; it means maturing and learning with it as if it were your baby. If you have decided to start, I recommend that you go back, as I explained at the beginning, and look for your passion without thinking about money at this moment. Don't worry; that money will come if you do what you have to do to start a business correctly. Now, focus on thinking about what feeling it would give you when delivering a quality product. Think about what people want or need that you can give them with your experience and talents. See if you are preparing in the areas where you need the most help. I advise you not to waste time; life moves very fast.

You can be happy using all your gifts, all your qualities, all your strengths to move forward. If you have them and you are doing it very well, this is part of happiness and satisfaction, that which comes from your inner being by being able to be productive in your goals, that which emerges when we say to ourselves: "I do something good." This helps you get started now and shift to a way where you motivate yourself to get started and move forward in life faster and further.

If God gave you those talents and made you for the purpose that you feel is strong in your heart, don't let it go; don't let that illusion die. He gave you that gift so that you could survive in this life, and he will never abandon you. I tell you this from my own experience and with the conviction that having faith and hope works. Trust that He will protect your business and bring you the right clients, the right people, and the ideal people so that your business is good, fruitful, and productive for your family and your employees. Take time each day to pray before each project or before starting your day so that you are certain when faced with any important decision. Ask your maximum power to give you the ability to satisfy your clients so that a quality product comes out of your business. It works to pray so that you can analyze your personality and have the wisdom to understand the path you decide to take and thus reach the goal.

When you finish, to know you better, give yourself a personality and career test on the internet. Many questionnaires are free, and they will help you before deciding to start your business or confirm what you have to work to get started. This is also a responsible step of action. Know yourself, educate yourself, and find what your personality is good at and why. These analyses are very good because sometimes we think we are good at something, and suddenly, we discover that we are better at something else. This also gives you more security to start now.

It is very normal for us to doubt ourselves when we do not know ourselves, and sometimes, the opinion we have of ourselves is not real. When we have our talents hidden, either because of incorrect messages that have been sent about us or because of negative experiences, it is likely that even the people we are closest to, do not know us, do not know how we think, or what our hearts are like. Sometimes, our loved ones believe and make us believe what we are not because they did not live the experiences that we lived before.

I invite you to start today with a clean state of mind. I invite you to fall in love with the person you are today, no matter the damage, the past, or what we were. Let's reinvent a new facet of admiration for ourselves, of trusting in who we are without anyone giving us wrong labels. Your greatest strength is not words; it is action that determines how you act and who you are.

I know it's not easy; it's a challenge, but action should only come from you, from how much you know yourself. Only you have the strength to fulfill your dreams, which do not necessarily have to be the same as those of others. Action is your own decision, and you cannot blame others for what you have not put action into achieving.

Focus on your goals, make them as big as you can, and make sure your mind has no limits. Don't feel guilty for believing in yourself; you need every grain of sand you can give yourself to motivate you to start. Manifest with your mind in abundance. Believe me, do this exercise and enjoy it; it feels good to do it. Look again for your list of strengths and weaknesses. Knowing your weaknesses makes you stronger because you will know what to work on. Be sure to review the solutions again next to the weaknesses.

Put action into having humility, always having the mentality of growth, the humility to look at yourself and recognize that we are not perfect and that if you do not have prosperity and abundance today, perhaps it is because something is failing. Could it be that you fail to understand the person in need? That person in need may be the one helping your business, but remember that if it were not for the people, we would not be able to have a business. Every business depends on people. Without clients, we are nothing. Thanks to them, we can generate jobs, fulfill obligations, and have consumers. By treating people badly, we do not achieve any successful relationships. Ignoring a client when they need you doesn't work.

Do you fail because of your absolute waste of time, your laziness, your health, your anxiety, your negativity, your lack of gratitude, or your influences? Do you have someone negative around you who is weighing their opinion more than what you are? Do you tell your dreams to someone without vision that affects you, to someone with envy? Are you living a purposeful plan, or is it a selfish plan? Do you want to help others with your product, or do you only think about money? Are you in debt for pleasure? All of this happens a lot, and it is a big obstacle for startups. That is why it is important to know them, because it is a reality that occurs every day, and the problem is not that it happens; the problem is that it affects us and that we do not look for solutions, knowing that we cannot change anything externally, but for ourselves, we can.

What do you need to get started? Faith? Do you trust that everything is going to be okay? Find a positive way of looking at things. People take action only in what they are convinced is right. Starting any project now with strong foundations of prosperity requires that you look at what gets you ahead and ignore what does not suit your business.

Knowing the obstacles is very important, as it can affect your blessings and prosperity. The attitude with which you face problems and how you solve them, focusing only on the solution, is something to which you should pay special attention.

Seeking to blame others doesn't solve things, focusing on destructive criticism doesn't work, it doesn't work when there are conflicts, resistance is high, and no one listens. On the contrary, pay attention to constructive criticism expressed by calm people in a pleasant and peaceful environment.

Steps to Start Strong

It is worth undertaking. DO IT!

Below, I share a list of some steps or stages that you must follow to start your business. Make a mark on the **box** and celebrate every time you complete one.

☐ **I discovered my natural gifts and new abilities.** Not everyone has what it takes to start a business, and that does not mean that your idea is not brilliant, but perhaps you are missing some necessary and natural personality characteristics to start a company. Before investing time or resources in your business, evaluate yourself and see if you have the typical characteristics of an entrepreneur, as well as analyze—as you learned at the beginning—what your purpose, your potential, and your motivation are.

☐ **I developed an idea.** Don't start a business just because it's something a lot of people are doing. Some people start projects, even though they don't like them, just because they see that someone else is making money with them. Do not do that. On the contrary, develop a business concept that you are passionate about, that creates emotion in your heart, that you feel, and that you use your talents to help customers. This is related to something you have some experience in, if possible, or innate talents that you need to improve.

Then, think back to a product or service that you think
will improve people's lives.

☐ **I follow what I believe firmly.** Once you have the
idea, find out how you can make it a reality. Is the
product something people want or need? Would you
buy it if you weren't the owner? Can you make a profit
by selling it? Do you have a purpose for the product?
Does it work?

☐ **I developed a strong business plan.** That is your map
of goals, missions, opportunities, and projections, which
will guide you forward. This plan is essential, and you
may need it in the future to present your ideas and goals
to investors. This plan, apart from the aforementioned
mission, must have an objective, a description of the
company and how the service or product works, what
is the market you want to reach, what are the financial
plans, how much capital is there, how much needs to be
invested, and how much are the estimated profits for the
next few years with operating costs.

☐ **I know my market.** Even if you have detected
some interest in your business, you need to do more
homework. Evaluate the market so that you sell to
the people who are sure to make the purchase. Do a
competitive evaluation.

☐ **I have determined the expenses.** Do additional
research and learn about common costs within your

chosen industry. Not only will this help you run the business more efficiently, but it will help you be more realistic about what you need to earn to make it work. It is not the one who sells more for the sake of selling and ego; it is the one who is doing a good business where there are results. This will also be very valuable information for investors in the future.

☐ **I found the right capital, banks, or investors.** The positive thing about starting a service-based business is that your need for investment capital may not be as high, and you may not need financial help. Otherwise, you're going to need some type of loan to get started, whether from your savings, credit cards, banks, donations, or family gifts. If you need it (**hopefully not**), find a partner for your venture who shares your passion, your ideals, and what you want to do, especially someone with a temperament that you think you can work with. These decisions can greatly affect the direction of your business if something becomes impossible. You can also find support in credit unions, which are nonprofit entities that promote the well-being of their members by returning profits in the form of reduced fees and lower loan rates. Members often have common interests and values when participating in an institution designed to help other members. Why do people sometimes choose a cooperative in different countries? Because, like banks, cooperatives accept deposits, make loans, and offer a wide variety of other financial services, but as cooperative and member-owned institutions, they provide a safe space to save and borrow at reasonable rates. Additionally, credit unions can provide financial education and assistance to consumers, branches within schools, and services for small businesses.

☐ **I have a marketing budget as a basic objective.** Once you determine how much money you will have to work with, figure out how much you need to develop your product or service and create an advertising plan. What will you use? ¿ *Social networks, flyers, mail advertising*? Will you work with advertising agencies? I recommend that you first exhaust all the free and available forms of marketing and then continue to a higher level if you need it or are not good in those areas, but whatever form you decide to use, do not leave that area uncovered since marketing is essential for your business.

☐ **I have calculated my earnings correctly**. Many people earn commissions on sales and face the challenge of moving their businesses and their families forward without being sure of how much they will earn each month. That is why they must create a budget without resting until they can advance at least six months of expenses. Doing this will help you have peace and stability in the process since the budget should be projected based on realistic profits.

> *"There is profit in all hard work, but*
> *endless talk leads only to poverty."*
> — **Proverbs 14:23, CSB**

Chapter
SIX

OVERCOME OBSTACLES WITH GRATITUDE

Trinidad worked a lot on her venture, a business she started with the goal of having more time for herself and her things, working from anywhere in the world, enjoying her life to the fullest without asking permission, and earning money while being free.

However, as time went by, she realized that none of that was happening, and she stopped feeling grateful for what her business had given her. Her own decisions led her to not have a balance in her life, and she no longer saw all the benefits of having a business. Even though her work sometimes brought her adrenaline and satisfaction, she was tired of working so much and didn't know how to separate her fun from the business. She had lost focus.

But one day, this brave entrepreneur said: "Stop!" and returned to search for her initial purpose. She understood at that moment that if she did not achieve balance, not only could she lose her health due to so much stress, but she could lose everything. It was the business she loved, but she was losing herself within it. So, she decided to take a vacation to make changes in her life and it worked.

Trinidad decided to visit Miami. While sitting in an open-air restaurant in the beautiful city, she began to see how people walked slowly, relaxed, and without worries. Men and women passed in front of her, ready to conquer the world, and some others, ready to rest.

After a delicious dinner, she began to walk slowly, breathe deeply, and see an opportunity to live and enjoy her life more. She analyzed with satisfaction everything that happened to her while she saw people smiling. With each step, her perspective changed as she reflected on how lucky she was to be able to move, run, scream... and, above all, live. She then began to thank herself for allowing her to enjoy this moment.

She was grateful for the properties that she was able to buy thanks to her business, which today generates income. She was grateful for her business, for everything she was able to do, and for everywhere she was able to travel. She was grateful for having an income that helped her cope with moments of illness, loneliness, or sadness. She was grateful while realizing how beautiful life was and that she had too many things to enjoy and be happy. She was grateful and, at the same time, nostalgic because she began to notice that her work addiction had become a way of entertaining her mind to cover up those things that she had to solve inside. She couldn't stop thanking God for giving so many years to her parents, two wonderful human beings who were no longer alive but who were always there. It saddened her deeply that they were not physically there, their absence hurt, but she thanked them with all her heart for the love and support she always received.

At that moment, Trinidad began to free herself from painful memories that she wanted to leave behind and that, without realizing it, had become a "thorn in the side" in her days of productivity.

From then on, the history of Trinidad began to change. Gratitude was the tool that led her to overcome what was hindering her and to change pain for peace. By being calmer and happier, she was able to move forward and be more productive, finding the balance that led her to achieve her goals and get up in moments of fatigue.

And you will say: 'But why are you telling me this story?' The answer is simple: because gratitude is one of the keys to progress. It happened in Trinidad's life and business, and it can happen in yours, too.

The life of an entrepreneur is not easy since there are so many obstacles and temptations that can lead to failure. Making a wrong decision can ruin much more than just the business; It can ruin the entire life, family, health, emotions, economy, and future, even of the next generation. But, above these difficulties, it is possible to lead a balanced life.

Having a balanced life means delegating fair time to each area: work, relationships, spirituality, hobbies, well-being, and personal care, giving each of them the importance and respect they deserve. Respect for what? To your motivation, to your initial value, to your purpose, to your why, to your time, to your values, to your dreams, to your ideals, to the people you work with, and above all, respect for yourself. That respect will lead you to not choose something temporary that will lead you to lose what you have worked so hard for and will help you to be consistent with what you one day promised yourself.

It is also necessary to clarify that there are stages in which the sacrifice is greater, and it is difficult to maintain balance, especially when you are starting. These are stages where the good and the bad mix easily and in which it is necessary to maintain focus. During that time, you will possibly lose activities, events, invitations, and even friends who cannot understand you. Still, you must be aware that this is okay and that sometimes it is necessary, as it will lead you to identify who those genuine friends are who want the best for you and that they deserve to be by your side. These times of temporary sacrifice help you enjoy a full balance of hope in the present to be able to enjoy prosperity in your future.

It's not easy to overcome obstacles, but it's worth it! It can be very stressful, and those stages of sacrifice will demand all your time and attention, but you will cope better if you organize yourself and take it one step at a time. At first, as you learn and structure, you may feel overwhelmed, but remember to use the tool of gratitude: be grateful while you inform yourself of the legal requirements, while you draw up a plan, while you establish how you will do your accounting, while you prepare your website or your social networks while you define the training of your workers. Once you learn and follow your structure, you will feel that everything becomes easier and easier. I assure you that it will be a great experience, personally and professionally.

Stories of Power

Some time ago, together with my team, we began the project of producing a pilot television program in which we told stories of improvement, intending to help people and entire families overcome difficulties and thus be able to achieve their dreams. It was a great challenge for us because it involved looking for sponsors, defining settings, decorations, lights, equipment, and music, writing scripts, and organizing logistical issues, among many other matters requiring time and effort. However, our driving force was thinking about what we would achieve and all the people we would help. We are grateful for being able to get a TV pilot, which was impossible to achieve for many.

There were many truly inspiring stories, but I want to tell you about one of them:

- Jacqueline, a woman who did not treat her emotions in time and whose severe depression had not allowed her to move forward, led her to lock herself in a world in which the four walls of her house were the refuge to escape from the dark life she had. Her situation was so complex that she became ill, lost her spirit, and stopped being herself. She knew that she needed to have her business because she needed income, and no job would understand her episodes of depression, but she was afraid. She didn't want to seek professional help and had simply resigned herself to not fulfilling her dreams. Jacqueline was sick and desperate. Upon meeting her, we felt that, despite her problems, deep down, she did want to get ahead and that we could help her be strong. She needed support, motivation, and business education, that is, advice aimed at promoting the fulfillment of her short and long-term goals with the resources she had, and that is what we did.

We helped Jacqueline find professional help, and thanks to her efforts and the support of those around her, the doctors began to see her change. With a lot of help, Jaqueline moved forward. She found a way to help others with her business and became motivated by organizing her schedule as it suited her so she could continue prioritizing her recovery. She began to have freedom, motivation, and faith, and her people also supported and understood her, being willing to listen to her when she was not well.

Jacqueline overcame her obstacles with gratitude and a good attitude and was able to move forward. She put the complaint aside, and she began to feel grateful for all those family members and professionals who wanted to help her. She began to give thanks for everything, and every day before going to sleep, she found more than ten reasons to thank God as a daily routine. She understood that she could move forward and give the best to her clients. What's more, her business began to do so well that she was able to find an employee to lean on during the times when her body and mind asked for rest and balance. His story is admirable.

Before we continue, I want to take a moment to talk about one of the most common obstacles on the path to entrepreneurship, and that is depression. Sadly, thousands of people are in deep need of help, internally screaming: "I can't take it anymore." Famous and "ordinary" people are battling with this inner enemy, which can be accompanied by anxiety and another series of emotional illnesses.

According to the manual *Diagnosis and Statistics of Mental Disorders DSM-5*, published by the American Psychiatric

Association[2], "signs and symptoms of clinical depression may include the following:

- Feelings of sadness, desire to cry, emptiness, or hopelessness.

- Outbursts of anger, irritability, or frustration, even over minor matters

- Loss of interest or pleasure in most or all usual activities, hobbies, or sports.

- Sleep disturbances, such as insomnia or sleeping too much.

- Tiredness and lack of energy, so even short tasks require greater effort.

- Lack of appetite and weight loss, or more food cravings and weight gain.

- Anxiety, nervousness, or restlessness.

- Slowness in reasoning, speaking, and making body movements.

- Feelings of worthlessness or guilt, fixation on past failures or self-reproaches.

- Problems thinking, concentrating, making decisions, and remembering things.

- Frequent or recurrent thoughts about death, suicidal thoughts, suicide attempts, or suicide.

2 REF

- "Physical problems without an apparent cause, such as back pain or headaches."

If you have some of these symptoms that do not allow you to move forward, if depression is your obstacle, visit your trusted doctor and seek help urgently. Only a professional can determine a diagnosis, but you must look for the reason for your discouragement and understand that even in the darkest moments, with help, you can heal and move forward. Depression is a place where if you don't get out of it quickly, it absorbs you, and it becomes increasingly difficult to escape, but you can get out of it. It's a long stretch, but it has an end if you work for it and you look for help.

Every dark moment brings problems; however, the hope to move forward and the desire to change must be much stronger. The light in your life will come thanks to the help of others, but mainly to your self-help and decision. Some specialists say that if an adult does not want to be helped, there is nothing anyone else can do.

No matter what you have, soul, spirit, and faith are essential to your business, your career, your financial prosperity, and your overall well-being. Don't let yourself fall. Think that you can do it and that you are equipped to do it.

If you feel alone in this fight, there are thousands of support groups in churches, in centers, and on the internet itself. Investigate, don't settle for; look for a purpose in this difficulty because maybe your experience will help others get out of the same thing. Away with depression, get up now, and live your dreams!

There is no problem so big that it has no solution. If God is with you and you are with Him, there is no eternal loneliness that cannot be replaced with good people around you. Choose your support group well. Always remember that it is possible. Repeat it a thousand times, even if you don't believe it. It will stay in your subconscious and will finally become actions. Come on, repeat after me: "Yes, I can. I am grateful because I can. I appreciate what I have. Everything will be fine. Everything will be fine."

Harbor's Story:

Fulfilling the desire to continue with your business without leaving family life

Harbor was a businesswoman in her forties with a deep desire to be a mother. It was a feeling she had long dodged to avoid disappointment with something she had no control over, so she didn't intentionally seek it out. What she didn't know is that at the time the desire became much more intense with the the idea of having a baby, she was already pregnant. When she realized it, she couldn't believe it. Kneeling, she cried and thanked God for that great gift. She begged for health and wisdom to take care of him and herself to protect him.

At that moment, she thought: "This is my family's time to feel and enjoy my son's life." She knew that the business model that she had built with so much effort could allow her economic stability, but at the same time, she was aware that she needed to continue fulfilling her responsibilities. Now she had to work much harder so that her son was well and she could continue with the standard of living and economy she had already achieved.

As it was a high-risk pregnancy due to her age, at first, she had many concerns. She thought about how devastating it would be to lose her son, but she held onto that life and overcame the worry with faith and action. She decided that she should take maximum care of her health, she should eat well, check herself with the doctors, and also meditate to take care of her heart, her soul, and her spirit. Her son became one of the most important reasons in her life to continue fighting.

Harbor knew that if God had sent her son, there was a purpose and that everything was going to be okay, but she also knew that in her business, she had responsibilities that she had to manage. So she decided to write down everything she should do in the business, to help others to manage and help her with her duties. She wrote about what she could do without affecting her new family situation and what things she should delegate. She understood that the business was a responsibility, a dream, a way to produce money for her family, even when she could not work, and despite the difficulties that the situation presented, she saw the positive, understanding that her business was also an instrument to help other people, giving them work. Therefore, among the measures she took was to extend the hours of her employees (a measure that made them happy since they would earn more), and she trained them so that they could cover what she was in charge of at that temporary stage she could not do. This way, she was able to get through her pregnancy happily and successfully without neglecting her business. Harbor was enjoying her experience.

Now I want to open a parenthesis in history to talk to you because only you can understand your situation, seek solutions in time, and not drown in difficulties. And maybe you think: "Yes, but she had more time in her business, and she was able to pay employees extended hours; I haven't reached that level." And yes, it is true, getting to that point requires time, wisdom, perseverance, and struggle, but everything becomes easier if you have the passion for doing what you like and if there is organization, savings, and good administration to be prepared when the times come. Harbor managed to move her business forward with a good team full of good people willing to work, but before achieving this, she had difficulties and was on the verge of giving up.

What I want you to see is the advantage of having your own business: over time, you can have a financial income to be okay if life presents you with situations in which you cannot work, such as an accident or an illness, or where you need to pause—like in this case, a family wish.

Do you think it was easy for her? Believe me not, because, with her new family as a priority, she also had stages in which her heart and spirit were tired. Not everything was fun and games, and as a human, she also had many weaknesses. But how did she manage to get out? That's what I'm going to tell you:

The first stage of Harbor was successfully completed. But life is not perfect, and despite the financial abundance, after pregnancy, she wrote a letter expressing what she felt when she could not sleep well due to having so many responsibilities and not finding enough support to move her business forward as quickly as she needed. This is what the letter said:

"I feel very sad, very lost, directionless, and ungrateful. Why do I feel this way if I have so many blessings and if my business is producing to the point of needing more staff? I don't know, but I feel bad. I want more time to take care of my son, and I want to share more with him, with my treasure, my grain of sand, and my life. I'm not enjoying pushing my company so hard with so much effort. I'm tired of hiring people who don't want to work. I put so much effort and devoted so much time to preparing others and helping my team improve; in the end, they didn't even appreciate it. I can't find the staff with the characteristics I need, and I am very, very frustrated. I need more help."

As many of us have experienced, Harbor was going through a moment of frustration when faced with the obstacle of making efficient decisions that would allow her to combine her work and personal life. She was feeling defeated by a temporary obstacle that had a solution and that she did not see.

Any business that grows is going to face these types of obstacles. It takes a team, but sometimes the patience, faith, and perseverance to achieve it disappear. In Harbor's case, the fact that she had just had a beautiful baby was added to the fact that her hormones and fatigue did not allow her to have the right mindset to see all the positive things that were happening to her. At that moment, what she needed most and lacked most was gratitude and faith, so much so that she was on the verge of selling her business for much less than what she would earn if she stayed with it.

With the mentality of defeat that was besieging her, Harbor began to neglect her spirit, her soul, and her heart, letting her fears invade her with her own words of discouragement. She repeated to herself in frustration with her team: "I'm tired of not having time. I feel like I'm losing my freedom and my passion; I feel like I have to obey something that I like, that I enjoy, but that I have to count on more people to move it forward, and I feel bad because it takes years and years of work, but I feel that I am not obeying what I know I have to do. My health is no longer the same as before. It makes me sad to feel this way; it makes me sad to feel like a failure when I am not. My business is very good, but my mentality is not the same. I cannot lose such a prosperous business; it is a very good business, a business that has cost me many tears, work, my time, and now the time of my son and me. I feel like all that effort... for what? My son is my priority."

Her spirit was so tired that she didn't see that there were ways to obtain and enjoy a business and family. Daily time is limited, and there are stages in which we simply cannot be present, but our responsibility is that if we cannot perform a role in a company, we must find someone who can replace us in that area for the well-being of the business. Harbor continued to have a negative mindset regarding her business and was not seeing the positives; her gratitude for it was slipping. Let's see this example of how her mindset was hurting her.

Harbor wrote again:

"If I'm not going to enjoy all the money I've gotten in life, what's the point? I feel that no one around me, not even my family, values the treasure, and the opportunity that I am giving them. They don't want it, and they don't even know what they are missing with being able to enjoy themselves without going through what I went through. Everything will be lost while my health goes away with stress.

Nobody understands the sadness and what I feel in my chest every time an employee leaves when I invest a lot of time training and they don't go to work when the staff does not follow instructions, and on top of that, they leave angry. I'm tired and frustrated, and with all this, I don't feel like continuing.

I'm going to enjoy everything I've worked on. I have motivated myself to work so hard to leave my fruits to my relatives when I die, but they don't even want to work in my business. I work so that if something happens to me, everything is left for my family, but they don't want to fight with me; they don't want to work with me. They treat me like they don't care about me."

She was writing with pain and focusing more on humans than on God; she was not practicing the thought of doing her best without expecting anything from anyone, which is why she felt alone. She allowed negative situations and thoughts, which only interrupted her success, as often happens when you depend on others and do not cling to God to bring the right people into your life.

The absurd mentality of negativity that she had embraced did not let her see that all of this was temporary and solvable since her company could pay for adequate help that would allow her to enjoy her son and, at the same time, allow her business to continue running alone, as it was managed for many years. Finding the solution was a matter of attitude and action.

Finally, she decided to have faith, and the person with all the characteristics she was looking for arrived. She was someone who listened and quickly learned to accomplish all necessary tasks. The support problem in the office was already solved. Yes, it came at the price of paying more for help, but in her case, it was a blessing to be able to have someone else, and, thanks to her business, she could enjoy her family, recover her health, and feel satisfied and happy with the goals achieved. Once again, with gratitude, faith, and action, she overcame a common obstacle in business: when the work team is not fulfilling the necessary responsibilities.

Everything was great, moving forward like never before, and when Harbor recovered, she was able to dedicate much more time to her business and enjoy a healthy balance of work, family, and friendships.

However, obstacles continued to arise, this time from close people who were affecting her emotions. After a year, Harbor returned to having negative thoughts, as many business owners often experience when they feel they are struggling alone, invaded by the emotions that interrupt miracles.

After having a balance for a long time, Harbor began to feel that she was not controlling her emotions, that her voices were excessively negative, and that she did not see the positive in her business. She felt hurt by other family members but tried to understand her family without taking anything personally; however, it was affecting her emotions, which were also affecting her businesses, she was not thinking about all those friends who did love her as if they were family, for whom it was important to make her feel good.

In that moment of exhaustion, she only had one way, which was God and herself, and so she wrote once again, this time, a prayer:

"God, I can't do it alone. Please help me! Help me so that the people who come to me are the people you sent. Help me choose the right people in my life, bring me the right people to work with me, those who you know will follow my instructions at work and do their job well, and in doing so, give me peace and tranquility. Give me the wisdom to understand, forgive, and accept those who do not want to be by my side, especially if they are people I love. Help me set my sights

on you and not on the man so as not to feel confused by my emotions if I become disillusioned with them at any time.

Thank you for being with me in all my craziness and in all the risks in my businesses. Thank you for the success and abundance that you have allowed in my life. Thank you for giving me family, thank you for the clients, thank you for all the successes in my desire to fill my spirit with you. Give me strength to help people; give me dreams. Help me because my spirit is fading from so much stress, and my health is deteriorating. Help me overcome my feelings because when something happens to my son, I go into defense mode, and controlling my emotions becomes difficult for me. Help me understand and have complete control of them.

God, take away my guilt of feeling this way and give me peace. Help me to do what you want with peace. Fill me with you, guide me to feel you every day in my heart. God fills me with health and allows me to enjoy my life feeling good and happy. God, help me take strong steps and lead me to your plan. Amen."

She finished making her sentences and then began to use the technique of writing the problem and looking for solutions written in front of them. This was her list:

Worry:

Employees

Action: *Don't rest until you get the right employees.*

Result:

In less than a month, the person who caused her so much stress and whom she didn't dare let go, resigned. After many interviews and opportunities, the right person came to work, a person as if she was sent by God, diligent, grateful, and works with enthusiasm. The clients are happy, and so is she.

Worry:

Time for work and family.

Action: *Plan and choose battles.*

Solution:

- *She chose the best products to offer and made it worth the time invested. She decided not to continue with products that consume time and do not produce enough profits to cover them.*

- *She changed her work style, starting to go to the office only by appointment and working as much as she could from home to share more with her son.*

- *She increased working hours in the office, so she was able to generate more jobs and allowed others to generate more income. Although she could earn that, her business gave her enough money to do it.*

- *She sought more advanced management technology programs so she could work smarter and not harder making work more effective and faster for everyone.*

Worry:

She wanted more time with her son:

Action: *She sought help and had a balance to spend more time with him.*

Solution:

She found a school where she would have peace of mind in leaving her son with cameras to see him. She felt he was very small and wanted to see him more during her work time and with excellent teachers. She knows that her business will provide her with the money to pay for a place where, apart from all these benefits, the child can have extracurricular classes that he can also enjoy with other children. When her son was not in school, she wanted to spend as much quality time with him as possible. Also, she was getting more help with her business, allowing her to spend more time with her son.

These are just examples of how to change the reactions we have, even though we have strong emotions.

Remember: You cannot control obstacles, problems, or situations, but you can control how you react to them, taking care of your heart, soul, and health with gratitude and faith.

"Don't be afraid, because I'm with you; don't be anxious, because I am your God. I keep on strengthening you; I'm truly helping you. I'm surely upholding you with my victorious right hand."

— Isaiah 41:10, ISV

Reflect

- What pushes your heart to work daily toward your purpose?

_____

_____

- What have been your obstacles?

_____

_____

- What do you think you can do to overcome what is holding you back?

_____

_____

- Have you sought professional help if your sadness doesn't allow you to motivate yourself?

_____

_____

- Write down five reasons you can be grateful today.

_____

_____

If you create your business with the act of constant gratitude in mind, you will see its benefits, you will value what you have more, and this will make you feel more fulfilled and happier. When you work with the deep and sincere intention of helping all your clients and thanking them for choosing you, the fruits will come through the door of your business.

Chapter
SEVEN
PARALYZING FEAR.

Fear is reasonable and normal because, in its proper measure, it is a way to protect yourself. The problem is when that fear paralyzes, sows limiting ideas, and absurd obstacles that block the mind with the false reality that one cannot fight to win. At that point, fears prevent you from achieving what you are capable of doing. That is why we must fight against it, and the first step to overcome fear is to identify it.

I want to help you with the following exercise:

Write down ten of the fears that stop you from starting your business now. In this exercise, you can analyze and try to understand yourself as a person, and next to each fear, write down what you need to feel safe in the face of that fear and what the solution is. It changes the way you see things, and it is for your convenience.

	FEAR	SOLUTION
1.		
2.		
3.		
4.		
5.		
6.		
7		
8.		
9.		
10.		

If your fears, to begin with, are expenses, write down alternatives or something positive, for example,

FEAR	SOLUTION
1. I am worried about being able to cover expenses.	Have a reserve of at least six months.

This is just an example. In this way, you identify the fear and propose a solution.

Given that particular fear, make a list of the monthly expenses that your business entails and the estimated profits you would need to be able to assume your responsibilities well. If the fear is not being able to pay, it is understandable, but planning the solution shows your responsibility, which is very good.

Another important step that helps you face fears is to design a work plan where you write down what you need to do to start, including deadlines. For example, make a list of the legal requirements you must meet to open your business in the country you are in and set a date by which you must have everything ready. Write where you should go, what documentation you should provide, and how much the procedures cost. Organizing yourself and providing solutions will give you more peace of mind and allow you to see your processes without confusion.

Once you have your reservations and process the requirements, review your work plan again to now take action. Make a list of your prospects, those people to whom you are going to offer your products, and how you are going to contact them: friends, family, referrals, strangers, contacts on social networks. At this point, making an appointment with a marketing professional will help you move your business forward. Being prepared to be able to take the risk will give you more security to start with.

How wonderful it is to be able to know your fears and where they came from and thus be able to overcome them so that the past does not damage your present. Trying has a cost, and that is time, but what about if it goes well and you can multiply your investment? What if a miracle happens? What if the right people come to you as angels sent from God, and you can fulfill your purpose by helping many people with your business? It is better to try everything than to try nothing.

If, with that dream, you can help yourself and your family, thinking about a goal and a successful outcome will help you feel peace and overcome fear. You deserve the opportunity to take steps of freedom without fear of the unknown, acting with the hope of a better tomorrow. You deserve to be free from the ties that wouldn't let you progress.

On this path toward your new life as an entrepreneur, it is normal that you feel afraid of leaving a daily routine and apparent stability and comfort. And although it is fine to work for others, the question is: What are you spending your valuable time on in exchange? Are you happy with what you do? Are your fears stopping you?

I am going to ask you many questions now, but please take time to meditate on the answers:

Have people hurt you in the past and you don't feel safe to act? Did they tell you you couldn't do something and you believed them? Think about what experiences those people had that led them to convey their fears. They may have had moments of defeat or failure; Maybe someone stole their dreams too and is now simply reflecting on you a fear that can continue for generations. Do you need to heal that wound? Do you need to forgive? What's stopping you? Is it the fear of losing the comfort you have, of not feeling safe? Or are you afraid of commitment?

> *The reasons don't matter, the circumstances don't matter, the people who are transferring fear to you don't matter, the voices that tell you that you won't be able to do it don't matter. It also doesn't matter how unfair you think life has been to you, if you haven't had the life you wanted, or if you have frustrated desires. None of that matters because it* **is not too late to start facing your fears and embrace the success that is waiting for you.**

Finding the reason for your fears and how to overcome them is key to advancing with your purpose so that you don't get sick with anxiety thinking about the worst that could happen. There are people with great talent who are eager to get started but have many fears that lead them to mistrust. If this is your case, talking to a professional can help you overcome what is holding you back. They can guide you on how to overcome fears and traumas so you can start to be happy. Each case is different, but I recommend you start by forgiving yourself because you have taken away desired possibilities, intentionally or unintentionally.

If you know that this project is your goal, overcoming your fears will help you. It will help you become better and also help others beat them, especially the people on your team. For example, one of the fears in sales teams is the fear of rejection. You need to help them overcome it because if they don't, it can decrease sales and affect their income as well as yours.

Go ahead and try! And if you fall, shake yourself off and get up! It's okay. It's okay to fail sometimes. What can happen? May you be happy knowing that you tried, that you fought for your dream, that you grew as a person, and that you didn't stop progressing, developing, and growing, and that today you are better. Don't be like many who only look at how others succeed, frustrated because they do not have the life they were looking for or what they dreamed of.

A Story of Power

Lidia had been at her job for years, but the entrepreneurial spirit that she had hidden inside made her feel frustrated for not having her own business. She was full of insecurities; she didn't trust people or have faith in anything, nor did she believe in anything stronger than her, that could protect her. She was afraid, a fear that began in her childhood.

When Lidia was little, she experienced two strong situations of abuse from which she could not escape and in which not even her parents could defend her. At that moment, she felt unprotected and assumed within herself that if she had not been able to take care of herself, much less would she be able to take care of anything. Mentally, she did not feel capable of making intelligent decisions. Furthermore, she had a childhood filled with a lot of violence that caused her to fear conflict, which in her present made her avoid any confrontation or anything that would require her to solve a problem with a client, even in a friendly way. All her potential was being overshadowed by trauma and fear.

This situation hurt her a lot, affecting not only her dreams but also her relationships at work, with her family and friends, and even with her partner. She felt guilty for a situation that took her by surprise and that, in the innocence of her young age, she did not know how to handle it.

But, despite her fears, Lidia decided to do something in her present to change her future and sought professional help. Her therapist began to work on each of her traumas and taught her how to forgive herself and others, understanding that others also have the traumas that lead them to act incorrectly. She taught her to applaud herself for having gotten out of that situation, to forget her past, and to work on her present. It helped her recognize the nobility of her heart and also gave her tools to identify dangerous situations so she could avoid them.

Lidia began to heal, work on her self-esteem, and overcome her fears. Her entrepreneurial spirit came out of hiding, and after some time working on herself, she was able to take the steps to start her real estate investment business with the conviction that she could protect her business. Today, she has more than ten properties and lives off her income. Identifying her fears, facing them, and healing was the key to not allowing paralyzing fear to stop her from achieving her goals.

You are worth more than any strong moment, than anyone who has hurt you, than anyone who wants to take advantage of you. If you have identified with Lidia's story, think about how you can get rid of that pain. Unload your feelings, write about them, talk to someone you trust, and seek professional help, but do something to move forward and continue on your path without fear.

> "Do not be anxious about anything, but in every situation, by prayer and petition, with thanksgiving, present your requests to God. And the peace of God, which transcends all understanding, will guard your hearts and your minds in Christ Jesus."
> — **Philippians 4:6-7. New International Version (NIV)**

Did You Find the Doors?

Feeling secure with our action plan will be the door that will lead us to overcome our obstacles with gratitude and face our fears of undertaking. That way, we won't depend on being given a chance, and we will live healthier from the inside out. That power will be the lamp that will illuminate our path to success.

I can say this with conviction because what I lost one day—family, material goods, and so-called friends—God multiplied for me in abundance. I learned to start from scratch and rise with Him, to fall on my knees crying, and to know that without Him, I am nothing but that with Him, everything is possible. Without looking for it, I became an expert at falling and getting up, and if I had to start from scratch again, I wouldn't feel afraid because I knew He was with me.

Getting up again is a challenge, but If you make it possible, you can achieve all your dreams, even if you have to start TODAY. I am a testimony of that. The gratitude I feel to

God for lending me so much on this earth and allowing me to manage what is His and live the best I can with what He has given me is greater than myself. That is why I ask God to take care of my path, to protect me and my family from all evil and danger, and to continue humbly using me to help others get ahead, as today I want to help you with this book.

I was blessed to find the motivation to achieve my dreams, to not be afraid to try what I wanted, keeping in mind that whether it worked or not, I would live the experience as part of the adventure of a lifetime. I verified for myself that where I put my heart, passion, planning, positivity, and gratitude would help me overcome obstacles. I got used to thinking that even the bad things that happened to me had the purpose of protecting me from something worse or making me stronger for something bigger that was coming soon. I learned to believe that losing something often means having something better.

Undertake is a sacrifice that is worth it. Finding a good purpose has filled me with satisfaction, not only for the material, but for what fills the heart, because the material does not go to the other world, and learning to let go was essential for overcoming obstacles with gratitude. When I talk about letting go, I mean the feelings caused by people who hurt you—forgive with peace and pray for them for you to heal.

I had to start, and I started, and today, I continue walking, facing challenges that I never thought I could overcome. No matter what happened in the past, it makes me feel increasingly lighter as I find solutions that work.

You have already found the key that you had in your hands and you have gone through one of the many doors that you will find on your way. Some will open up and some won't, but if you continue, there is still a lot to learn. Cheer up, be brave! Go ahead, keep reading.

Part Three:
Keys That Open and Close Doors

Chapter

EIGHT
WINNING MENTALITY

ow that you have worked through the fear that paralyzes you, you must combat it with the right mindset. *In this chapter, you will find some of the tools you need to do it more easily.*

When you face the reality of entrepreneurship, it is normal that problems overwhelm you and lead you to see situations bigger than they are. But regardless of whether they are big or small, a winning mentality is one of the keys that opens the next door you need to cross to get ahead.

A positive mindset saves you energy, helps you not take anything personally, understands that situations happen, and helps you focus on the solution without anger, sadness, or frustration. This mindset facilitates the ability to face challenges and simply move forward with bigger and better plans. People with this type of mentality achieve a lot, as it is an amazing tool. Having a positive mentality allows them to even enjoy problems.

On the other hand, people who think that everything is against them get angry based on assumptions and suffer. They assume that people hate them, which causes a feeling of rejection in them. It is difficult for these people to move on; it is simply because they accept their negative interpretations of things as true. Fighting over a problem that only exists in the imagination is a strong poison for the soul, which only affects the person who experiences it. A negative mindset causes them to miss out on friends, jobs, and opportunities in life.

My invitation is that if you are struggling with that type of mentality, work to change it. How? Not assuming anything, communicating, asking instead of accusing, listening and understanding the why of things, and above all, making correct decisions only after analyzing situations with a real perspective and with confirmed arguments.

I want to tell you an anecdote about this:

When I first went to extreme poverty neighborhoods to help them open their businesses, as a volunteer in the community, I found a common factor that prevented many people from moving forward. It was not a lack of resources because, through volunteering, they were provided with the minimum equipment to open their small business so that they could help support their families; It was what they had built in their minds. Their argument was: "The rich are bad people."

Despite the scarcity, I heard excuses like: "Money only brings problems, and I don't want to complicate my life," "I'm too old to start," or "I'm too tired to do anything." They got used to thinking that living with less was better, even if that meant being out of work, having many children at home going hungry, being on the streets using drugs, sad, hopeless, empty, and without value.

I was shocked, hearing millions of complaints that would not end because they did not seek solutions. I didn't understand how they could think that when you use your talents, you don't feel tired. I didn't understand that way of thinking, especially if they needed money to solve many of their problems. Contrary to what they thought, their lives were becoming increasingly complicated by not being able to visit a doctor or not being able to buy food or medicine. If they needed the money, why did they think financial prosperity was bad?

I want to clarify that not all of them were like this, but the fear of progress and comfort in misery was common in their life stories in a neighborhood that they called bad and dangerous. The word fear was mentioned many times, as it was established and affirmed in their minds.

I don't know if you also experience something similar and if there are hidden feelings toward prosperous people, but if so, the first thing you should do is analyze what you feel when you see someone who is financially better off than you. So, instead of comparing yourself negatively, ask yourself and even investigate how that person came to get what they have, how she faced the difficult times, and how she used faith to keep going, even with pain in her body, mind, heart, and also analyze whether your mindset is positive or negative.

Changing your mentality about people with money will make you capable of taking advantage of great financial possibilities without any guilt about obtaining the results of your actions. Remember that people who see life positively solve problems faster.

Let's do a quick personal analysis exercise and answer the following questions honestly:

- When you see a successful businessman with a lot of economic prosperity, what do you think?

- Do you think there are bad and good people, whether rich or poor?

- Do you think you deserve to prosper?

- Do you think you should change your mentality? In what way and why?

- Do you think that with some defeatist comment, you are unintentionally affecting your prosperity and that of others?

- What do you think is the mentality of people who do not progress financially?

We must undergo a metamorphosis in which we recognize that although we are not perfect, we are one of those who want to transform into our best version in this life to be able to enjoy it. Let's believe that everything old that destroys us must go away, and let's focus on getting away from everything toxic, including our minds. I say this because our minds are also often toxic when we do not control them, when we continue to live from the memories of the past, dragging them into our present and allowing them to stop us.

I want to clarify that this does not mean that we cannot remember our past. That would be impossible because we all have a story in which we have experienced problems and all kinds of circumstances. Life is not easy; more happens to some and less to others, but when there are painful memories, we must urgently look for ways to heal them so that they do not stop us. For this, we have to be selective with whom we share our pain. Doing it with people who do not support us will cause more pain than we have, but if we go to someone capable of putting themselves in our shoes and stopping our mental exaggerations, we can find a different way of seeing problems, thus creating a positive and healthy within ourselves and our relationships.

As I have already told you, I am a person of faith, and for me, the first option to change my mentality and heal is to seek God and His Word and believe that He can connect me with the right people so that they can reach me, even If there is a need to seek professional help. I don't know what your belief or what your maximum power is, but feeling that protection is the key to moving forward requires a lot of effort because the only person who will obtain all the gains and benefits is you if you seek help and fight. Remember that the worse the problem has been, the more you will have to work, but in the end, you will find a solution to what has been bothering you, like a giant stone in your shoe.

"Indeed, I'll bring you healing, and I'll heal you of your wounds," declares the Lord [...]"
—Jeremiah 30:17, ISV

Life will always put many ways before us to solve different situations, but it is up to us to choose with the right mentality, always be open and willing to understand our experiences, and be flexible to change. This change consists of leaving behind our old ways of solving problems and finding new ones, analyzing if there were issues that did not work in the past; perhaps by making certain changes, we can move forward with a better spirit and a winning mentality.

People with a successful mentality, faith, and action lift others to the end and give even what they don't have, with passion in their hearts, believing that if God is with them, everything is possible.

Chapter
NINE

PUT FAITH IN
YOUR WORKS

W e are finding keys that help us open and close doors, and the first was to change the paralyzing mentality to a winning mentality. But if we want to open more doors, it is necessary to move from the mind to the spirit and then ask ourselves: how are we taking care of our spirit? What do we believe and trust? Who guides us?

One of the key habits for many successful entrepreneurs with a winning mentality is to fill their spirit with faith daily as an essential task. We all function differently, with individual beliefs that are respectable. We all have our convictions and sometimes the confidence to be able to give our opinion, even if it is different. Each person chooses whether or not they want to continue with what they were taught in childhood, added to what they have learned every day to build a better path.

Without my faith, I would never have been able to move forward because there were many possibilities of things going wrong, and it was very difficult to move forward without the hope that everything would be okay. That faith that drove and motivated me and continues to do so has allowed me to see how projects emerge and grow in amazing ways. I had miracle after miracle that today provoked deep gratitude for the results and no regrets for having had faith.

Trusting in the Holy Spirit becomes a light on the path because by seeking His help and guidance that illuminates us, we move with a firmer step, walk with more confidence, renew our spirit, change attitudes, and think much more positively. This is where we say it sticks to the branch of opening possibilities, of opening our minds and hearts, of waiting patiently for us to do our part. Faith is a powerful tool that helps us stay calm when we are worried, trust in promises, and rest in the knowledge that everything will be fine, thus enjoying the process.

It is time to remove fear, limitations, and prejudices against what you believe, ignore what people will say, and start fighting for what you want. Strive to please God by being disciplined, vulnerable, and empathetic without judging anyone. Dare to bare your soul before God so He can enter your heart and use you to help others with the talents He has given you. This way, you will have a lot of prosperity because money and abundance will come if you focus on helping.

Do what you have to do with firmness and discipline, and I know you will achieve it. You are not alone; it is simply us who turn away by not seeking professional help and by not trusting that God will send the right people. Trust that there is a time of divine formation, that there is hope, that there is light.

Designate a time to talk to God about the decisions you need to make. In every step you take, talk to Him as if He were a friend. Calm down. Get out all that you have in your heart. Sometimes, you are meant to be alone with God, like when He was in the desert, which became seasons of preparation for when **the destroyer tried** to damage him. The world is not perfect. Destructive people are going to approach you, and they will come like parasites to depend on you. What they seek is to set you back, but if you maintain a winning mentality and feed your spirit, they will not achieve it.

There are also times to simply dedicate yourself to yourself, your company, and your goals and to grow so you can help others get up and not fall. These are times to fly, thankful for everything God did, because remember: it is He who did it. Do not allow your ego to separate you from Him and everything beautiful He has for you. Do not allow pride to destroy you and lead you to your worst state. Get used to receiving prosperity and triumph with humility and gratitude, knowing that without God, you are and have nothing. Having Him is the most beautiful gift you can receive in this life; It is what allows you to get out of your problems, make decisions with clarity, and receive abundance in your life with the people around you.

Faith to Multiply

They were humble fishermen. They were tired and frustrated because they had worked all night without achieving what was the sustenance for their families. All their attempts had been fruitless, the nets were empty, and their strength had remained at the bottom of the sea until Jesus entered the scene. An instruction that seemed absurd, and the obedience of a man who acted in faith caused a miracle.

Whether you're a Christian or not, you've probably heard or read this Bible story, found in Mark 6:42-44, in which Jesus made empty nets that overflowed in abundance—a story with a message in which faith caused multiplication.

What message do I have for you based on this story? That God wants you to prosper financially. Just as you read it, God is interested in the resources you obtain from your effort and talent being multiplied, and with those resources, you grow and provide for others.

God saw the effort of a talented man and multiplied his results, bringing prosperity for him and provision for the people since that fish was sold in the market so that the people would have provisions and not be hungry. It was a win-win relationship:

the fishermen were earning by selling their products, and the people were earning by having food. The famous miracle of the multiplication of fish calls us to trust that when we offer our talents with a winning mentality and faith, God, with all his power, will make great things for us and will multiply our ordinary resources by doing extraordinary things.

God gives the same thing to many people, and each one chooses what to do with what he has. God gives them. In the Scriptures, the Lord gives us multiple examples where he shows us how to produce the expected return with everything He gives us in abundance. Biblical success then consists of working in the here and now, trusting that God always gives us what we need and more.

***Matthew** 25:14-30, **CSB** Tells us the parable of the bags of gold, or the talents, as it is popularly known. Read it with me in version:*

"14 "For it is just like a man about to go on a journey. He called his own servants and entrusted his possessions to them. 15 To one he gave five talents,[a] to another two talents, and to another one talent, depending on each one's ability. Then he went on a journey. Immediately 16 the man who had received five talents went, put them to work, and earned five more. 17 In the same way the man with two earned two more. 18 But the man who had received one talent went off, dug a hole in the ground, and hid his master's money. 19 "After a long time the master of those servants came and settled accounts with them. 20 The man who had received five talents approached, presented five more talents, and said, 'Master, you gave me five talents. See, I've earned five more talents.' 21 "His master said to him, 'Well done,

good and faithful servant! You were faithful over a few things; I will put you in charge of many things. Share your master's joy.' **22** *"The man with two talents also approached. He said, 'Master, you gave me two talents. See, I've earned two more talents.'* **23** *"His master said to him, 'Well done, good and faithful servant! You were faithful over a few things; I will put you in charge of many things. Share your master's joy.'* **24** *"The man who had received one talent also approached and said, 'Master, I know you. You're a harsh man, reaping where you haven't sown and gathering where you haven't scattered seed.* **25** *So I was afraid and went off and hid your talent in the ground. See, you have what is yours.'* **26** *"His master replied to him, 'You evil, lazy servant! If you knew that I reap where I haven't sown and gather where I haven't scattered,* **27** *then[b] you should have deposited my money with the bankers, and I would have received my money[c] back with interest when I returned.* **28** *"'So take the talent from him and give it to the one who has ten talents.* **29** *For to everyone who has, more will be given, and he will have more than enough. But from the one who does not have, even what he has will be taken away from him.* **30** *And throw this good-for-nothing servant into the outer darkness, where there will be weeping and gnashing of teeth.'"*

Having prosperity is not bad, or how you decide to manage it; the important thing is that you are aware that our actions always have a consequence, whether good or bad, and we will reap our fruits because God will always give more to people who multiply what He gives.

Reflect

- For you, what is the biblical meaning of multiplying?

- Do you think you have made an effort to cultivate for the difficult times?

- Have you used your talents with a winning mentality and faith?

When God established commands for us, He did so not for the sake of it but because He was thinking about our protection and well-being. Many of them are not easy, but I encourage you to put all your efforts and faith in your works in their hands so that you see the multiplication in your life and your business project.

If you are interested in getting ahead, organizing your finances, and seeing your businesses prosper, you have to take steps, and while you get there, enjoy the process. Stay, surrender to Him, ask Him all your concerns, change your way of thinking, pray, and wait patiently. God loves you and protects you and will not let you fall. You are His son, His darling, His daughter, His wonderful creation, and He wants the best for you, but He always respects your decision because He gave you free will to use it.

If you want to progress and you want to do all this, you will achieve it, but if that is not what you want—if you do not want to do anything or be in Him—it is also your decision. We all have different paths, and this is only one life option.

If you are confused and don't know where to start, I suggest two simple steps:

1. Make a list of your goals financially and spiritually. It doesn't matter if you think they are small or insignificant or if, on the contrary, you think they are unattainable; just bring them to God with organization. Write the solution or plan next to each goal and trust Him.

2. Repeat this prayer:

   Lord, I am ready to open my heart to you, to learn from you, so that you guide me to obey you. Lord, help me in those areas that hurt me. I give you all my emotions. I need to have you close in moments of trial and crying but also in joys and triumphs. I put in your hands, my business, my family, my current or future employees. Multiply my efforts, my finances, my resources. Help me to put faith in your word and find in me what I need to prosper in all areas and thus be able to help others. Thank you for allowing me to be close to you. In the name of Jesus, amen.

Congratulations! You have taken a big step. That does not

mean that everything will be easy and perfect for you because, amid our imperfections, certain things will be more difficult for you to follow, but He knows your heart. God knows that everything you are doing is to get ahead and build your business so that your family and the people around you do well.

It's time to see what you are and have and not what others say about you. Believe what God says you are. If He made you and gave you all your talents, it is because He knows you and knows what you are capable of. You are on this earth to fulfill a giant purpose. Just manage your mind, your emotions, and your will so that you have a soul full of abundance and security for your businesses. Trust that everything will be okay in the midst of any experience or process of change. Good things come for you if, in your soul and your decision, you take firm steps.

Move forward, put faith in your works, and let God show you how His power is perfect in your weakness.

Chapter
TEN
LAZINESS AND BUSINESS

Beware of laziness!

From a very young age, we have heard that being lazy is not good for us and that laziness is "the mother of all vices," but have you ever thought about how much laziness could affect your finances? Lazy people want to reject everything that represents extra work, and in the case of their savings, sometimes the same thing happens to them. For example, a lazy person prefers to stay at the same bank to avoid the fatigue of withdrawing money and opening an account at another, even if that means higher interest or losing benefits. Therefore, laziness is not convenient in any area of life, even less so when it comes to your finances and business. You need to understand that you must get rid of it to see your finances grow.

Below, I will present several definitions and quotes, some biblical and others not, that better illustrate this concept:

- The dictionary defines laziness as a "lack of inclination to action or work."

- Proverbs 6:4-11 defines laziness and advises observing the diligent and cautious work of the ant so as not to have to pay the consequences of an unproductive life.

- The French writer, poet, playwright, and literary and theater critic. Jules Renard said: "Laziness is nothing more than the habit of resting before being tired."

- Proverbs 19:15 says, "A lazy person sleeps so much that he ends up hungry." Wanting to continue sleeping, seeking only a nap or a rest, and crossing your arms so as not to work has fatal consequences, especially in the economy. Forgive me if I scare you, but if you are like that, you may end up in the most terrible poverty since laziness is its root. It is one thing to rest because you need it, you want it, and you are already productive, everything needs a balance. After all, you earned it because you deserve to enjoy yourself after a productive time or for health reasons, and it is quite another to do nothing out of laziness and having needs at the same time.

- The Bible greatly exalts activity and work. In Noah's case, he spent years building the ark. If he had been lazy, he would have built a small boat and taken the most beautiful and even incomplete animals just for convenience. So today, we wouldn't be telling the story.

Indicators of a Lazy Person

- A lazy person always finds excuses not to do his job, and often, they are meaningless.

- The lazy person has bad relationships and irritates those who have to support him because it is not easy to want to help someone who does not want to help himself.

- The lazy person spends his time hoping that luck will help them: "If it comes, good, and if not, also good." They live waiting for the magical day when the phone rings with the great news that changes their finances or when an envelope arrives announcing that they have won things without working for them. They don't have in their minds the idea that they have to work for their destiny, that they have to fight for their financial freedom, that they have to create their wealth.

- The lazy people are expert procrastinators and always put off until tomorrow what they can start doing today. With this, I do not mean that it is wrong to plan for the future, but the future begins to be built today, step by step, laying brick by brick to build your life the way you want.

Laziness leads you to lose money quickly

• **Laziness to work on your prosperity**

The lazy person fails to achieve abundance due to his negligence in neglecting the resources he has.

— Proverbs 24:30-31, ESV

"I passed by the field of a sluggard, by the vineyard of a man lacking sense, and behold, it was all overgrown with thorns; the ground was covered with nettles, and its stone wall was broken down."

— Proverbs 27:23-27, ESV

"Know well the condition of your flocks, and give attention to your herds, for riches do not last forever; and does a crown endure to all generations? When the grass is gone and the new growth appears and the vegetation of the mountains is gathered, the lambs will provide your clothing, and the goats the price of a field. There will be enough goats' milk for your food, for the food of your household and maintenance for your girls."

• **Laziness in having a purpose**

It may seem strange, but the desire to collect without purpose, without helping, and without good intentions is called greed and may lead to poverty. Many people who want to have more invest in the wrong places, where they end up being scammed because they become blinded.

Sometimes, for the lazy person, money can become an end and not a vehicle to achieve things other than money. Saving is a good practice, but it should be with a good purpose so that it can multiply faster, knowing that a great purpose will allow you to enjoy the process.

> *"Doing right sets honest people free, but people who can't be trusted are trapped by their greed."*
>
> **— Proverbs 11:6, ERV**

> *"Greedy people hurry to become rich. They do not know that they will soon be poor."*
>
> **— Proverbs 28:22, EASY**

It is one thing to be diligent and feel satisfaction when achieving a goal, and another is desperation, thinking anxiously and making quick decisions without thinking them through or letting material things take away your peace. If this happens, your concentration is not on your purpose; the focus is the love of money. If this is the case, you may be limiting your abundance without enjoying the process of success, and it may be the reason why you are not motivated. You have to learn to let go.

- **Laziness in choosing well who you associate with**

Much money has been lost due to inappropriate and reckless associations without analyzing how important they are. A partnership is like a marriage, and your business is like a baby. Proverbs exhort us to avoid people who lead us to misery. Think carefully about how you relate, what decisions you make, and why you chose the people in your business, your partner, and your partners.

Don't let the desperation and laziness of not taking the time to analyze affect you to the point that you give part of your business to someone who could ruin it or make your life more difficult. Progress is associated with peace and harmony because problems will come, but what depends on that positive spirit is that you can solve them appropriately.

- **Laziness in making good decisions**

It is very good to live well because if it can be done comfortably and without worries, why not do it? But we receive this through the decisions we make.

Two factors that lead to rapid poverty are waste and extravagance, which are caused by the lack of means to pay. If you have it and can comfortably indulge your tastes, do it without feeling guilty. After all, they are your tastes, and you have worked hard for them, but if you do not have the resources, it does not help to be irresponsible by making decisions just for pleasure.

Do not trust anyone to be your business partner, much less if that person has not proven to be responsible or does not have enough time to do so. You can get a lot of disappointments, frustrations, and problems.

"My child, be careful not to promise more than you can really do. You may have promised to pay the debts of a friend or of a stranger. ² Then what you have promised to do may become a trap that catches you. ³ Now you need to escape from your problem. Your friend has got power over you. So you must be humble. Go quickly to him and ask him to forgive the debt. ⁴ Do not let yourself sleep or even stop to rest until you have met with him. ⁵ You must make yourself free from the trap. Escape quickly, like a bird or a deer that runs away from a hunter."

— Proverbs 6:1-5, EASY

"Only a fool would promise to pay for someone else's debts."

— Proverbs 17:18, ERV

I hope this book helps you and your family with finances. The family is like a table, when one leg is missing, the imbalance makes it fall, causing destruction. Remember, it is our responsibility to help others grow together and progress more easily for everyone's convenience. You will see how, by helping and contributing to your family, you will progress, you will avoid resentments and problems, everyone will have more peace and a higher quality of life, and thus, together, you can work with a purpose to help others. We must keep in mind that if there is a person who is very giving but makes his family suffer, it is of no use because the price is very high and it is not worth it. If there is someone in the family who tries to live at a higher standard than they can meet, it unbalances the family group and sets it back. You have to be a little more careful and find a balance where everyone uses their strengths to help in areas where other family members are weak.

- **Laziness to help others**

Is it part of our progress to help the needs of the poor or less fortunate? People who are sensitive to the needs of others are always working to provide for those in need.

On one occasion, I went as a missionary to Africa, and it was a great experience; I saw a lot of need: children who were missing hands and feet, mutilated by their parents, children with mosquitoes on their faces all the time, children eating garbage in the street, but I never forget that they all had the best smiles I have ever seen in my life. I went to help without expecting anything in return, but I was one of the most helped people, spiritually and financially, because without looking for it, after that experience, unexpected doors opened for me.

After subletting for a long time the location for my business in Florida, God touched the hearts of those who owned the premises to accept me on the terms I needed and the amount I could comfortably pay while I was in Africa. For me and my possibilities at that moment, that was a miracle, which, without me asking for it, came as a result of generosity. That is what I felt.

After renting there for about another ten years, the doors opened again so that I could have my own place, and I could be the one who could sublet to others.

> *"If you help other people with your money, you will do well. If you give water to thirsty people, you will not be thirsty yourself."*
> — **Proverbs 11:25, EASY**

- **Laziness to manage your time**

If you want to advance and prosper, you need to be focused on managing your time and doing what you need to do without distractions. Why are you wasting time on personal matters during progress time when you should be working toward your dream?

If you work from home, that focus is even more important because there are more distractions, and you must stick to a schedule for yourself, without other responsibilities, television, or distractions, and even feeding and rest times must be planned. The time allocated to carry out your project is only for that, and you must be focused.

Your focus is what leads you to fulfill your dreams. Yes, you know that what you are going to do is good for you. When you execute it, don't even think about it; just do it, and that's it.

How to Boost Your Spirits and Be Free from Laziness

We are human, and it is normal for moments to come where distraction, comfort, demotivation, and what is easy and what is fun become temptations and obstacles to achieving our goals. That is why we must prepare well, stimulating our spirits without depending on anyone else, since our motivation is our responsibility.

I recommend that you ask yourself the following questions so that you can get to know yourself and find what stimulates you to action:

- Are you motivated to read?

- Do you watch motivational videos on the internet?

_____

_____

- Does listening to music activate you? What kind of music do you prefer?

_____

_____

- What activity activates your creativity, and what factors block you?

_____

_____

- Do you practice any sport?

_____

_____

Other good motivators can be:

- Thinking about the words of someone you know who lifts your spirits and stimulates your desire to move forward.
- Remember the person you want to fight for to provide.
- Picture yourself in your mind by doing what you like.
- Activate your faith.

Chapter
ELEVEN
HEALTH AND FINANCIAL PROGRESS.

Life often presents situations that are out of our hands, such as a genetic health problem or an accident, but if within what depends on us, we can take care of our health, why not do it? Why have the fruits of a business if we cannot fully enjoy them by being in bed?

The issue of health, both mental and physical, is very important because if we do not seek to be in the best possible shape, our businesses can collapse, among other things. After all, deteriorated health can be very expensive.

A neglected and weak body is reflected in neglected and weak business results.

The owner, CEO, or manager usually has many responsibilities, such as the person who manages the household finances or household responsibilities. A business can be packed with work and feel like a cardboard box, with no windows, no way out, no escape, and simply collapse.

Taking care of your health is one of your powerful weapons to enjoy all your efforts. That's in this chapter, and I want to talk to you about how crucial it is to lose the fear of discovering how your health is, to take responsibility to be better physically, and to fight so that you can have results in your company and quality of life, even if an unexpected illness comes to you. I cannot indicate specific solutions for you because that must be done by an expert in the health area who knows your case and tells you what you can do to feel better with more energy, what foods are for you, and which ones affect you, and how to enjoy your maximum potential. What I can do is push you to be the best you can be so that you can earn money and enjoy your family with health.

I want to tell you the story of Catherine, a prosperous business woman with a stable business during many years. She had an excellent team that worked well even though she wasn't there all the time. But due to health reasons and an unexpected accident, there came a time when she didn't know what to do with her life, and she was a little lost and in constant pain. She worked day after day, ignoring her problem until she was forced to have surgery and spent many days in bed.

It was a very difficult season, but she didn't even complain. Her family and her job helped her get ahead. With her professionalism, she was able to see the positive side of the matter and take the little work she could do as a source of entertainment after having to rest for so many days. Such was her attitude that, on many occasions, neither clients nor her employees realized what she was going through. She overcame her situation, and thanks to that, she returned to work with the mentality that without health, we are nothing.

Catherine discovered how fragile we are, and during her time of rest, she had time to analyze why and what to live for. It was no longer money that motivated her since she had already managed to live a whole life with it. It was her purpose, that reason, that helped her cheer up in the moments when her health did not allow her to be well. She learned to see life with more humility, paying more attention to what was important, which was not money, but how she used it, using her maximum potential.

While in bed, Catherine relieved her dreams and began to think about how and where she wanted to live from that moment on and how she wanted to manage her schedule so as not to have so much stress and maintain a balance since she worked too much. Seeing herself in that state clearly showed her that no matter how much she had help, no one that she knew while she was in bed was going to feel what she felt: loneliness, abandonment, frustration, worry about being sick. She even felt that it wasn't even fair for someone to stay there with her.

After that situation, she saw life differently. She already wanted to be well and do everything she stopped doing. She wanted to pursue her dreams, and she even began to imagine her ideal life. She realized that she had a beautiful real life that she wanted to enjoy. She set out to keep what she had and appreciate her present, seeing in it all the potential she had for "her crazy ideas" and receiving everything she had as a blessing and a purposeful gift from God. During her illness, she did not let what she had fall apart because the efficient way in which she had prepared her business allowed her to sustain it comfortably. Her fears of not having momentary health did not prevent her from being able to motivate herself again so as not to lose what she had achieved.

In her convalescence, Catherine decided to change her pace of life and thought about which people she wanted to spend more time with. She decided to work on the small details that help her well-being and health.

Her first action was to analyze her daily routine, which allowed her to see the positives of getting up early and having a business that would not limit her role as a mother. Getting up early would allow her son to get to school early and allow her to be there earlier for the employees. In addition, she established an ideal time to have breakfast and be able to eat something before starting the day, something she had not done before due to so much work.

Catherine also acknowledged that one of her biggest weaknesses was her eating and exercise habits. Being young and having a slim build, she did not care much about eating healthy or about including sports in her daily life. As a consequence, her health deteriorated not only because of the accident but because her muscles were weak and without energy. She acknowledged that she always complained about being very tired at the end of the day, that sometimes she ate something quickly or did not eat at all, and that the people around her easily noticed how her business was growing, but her health was fading because she did not have clear priorities. Then she admitted that she had to work on this area, even though going to the gym bored her, and that she had to organize herself to eat better. She decided to discipline herself and look for a physical activity that she liked that could help her keep her cholesterol and triglycerides at the correct levels since she was aware that this was affecting her health and that she was not doing much to solve it.

Valuing her health, she regained regular visits to professionals who helped her improve her physical, mental, and spiritual state since health was no longer a hobby but her priority. Thanks to her self-motivating personality, she decided to seek a better quality of life. She wanted to get out of bed with energy, look younger, and feel more full of life, and she started with small steps until she achieved a habit that she enjoyed. She was clear that if her health were not good, her performance in the business would be affecting her production. That conversation with herself revealed to her that if she is healthy, motivated, and energetic, her business will be healthy, too.

Catherine got active and achieved it... And you? What do you plan to do?

Your life is made up of many areas—health, finances, work, relationships, spirituality—but they are part of a whole that is you. Therefore, they all have to be strengthened because that way, if one area weakens, another can support those gaps. In the world of successful businesses, time goes by quickly, and the days fly by, but why have money if the other areas are not enjoyed?

Having a balance is possible. You can have and enjoy it all, but it requires effort, loving, motivating yourself to act, designing an effective plan for your health, and fighting for it. I know that it is difficult to find the time because half of the day is spent taking care of family, taking the children to school, managing the business, returning missed calls, organizing a list of activities, assigning responsibilities, giving training, and achieving objectives. Therefore, unless you intentionally make time for your health as if it were part of your business and your life, you are not going to achieve it.

I know it will take time to start and get used to doing it, but it is never too late because although we can't do anything with the past, with the present and the future, we can.

Self-control, Rest, and Learning to Delegate

Do you remember Trinidad? You read her story in Chapter 6, where I told you how she overcame obstacles with gratitude in the middle of a journey she had to take to rethink her business. I'm going to tell you now something else that she was able to reflect on at that time related to her health.

Trinidad, with her goal of being happy and overcoming obstacles to achieve it, sitting on her vacation, having a coffee, and looking at the panorama, analyzed how important physical health is, and how by working too much, not eating well, and not worrying about it, was deteriorating. As she stopped, breathed, and took the time to analyze everything that moved around her, she also saw elderly people running who looked in good health, which caught her attention. She admired and felt emotional seeing how people took care of themselves, and she didn't. Those people who were walking around during what were office hours for others had something she wanted to call *freedom*. Freedom to move, freedom to run, and freedom to set aside time for their hobbies in an environment where people seemed comfortable and happy. She saw how, when health is lacking, this also affects a business.

If you are one of the people who believe that this has nothing to do with your productivity, look at how people who abuse alcohol or any other substance behave. Do you think they are in their best condition, concentration, spirit, or sanity to handle your business? Do you think your clients would notice? This is not to mention that there is no shortage of those who did not have time to go home to change and decided to arrive with the smell of alcohol or other substances. I say this just to give an example, but any type of abuse by the owner or his employees affects the function. Always remember that vices and addictions consume money and time and ruin homes because when there is an addiction, it means that the person cannot stop and that they have no control.

And how does this affect your business? It affects you a lot because you need to have that personality of control, decision, health, and motivation, of cleansing in your being, of healing what needs to be healed for your well-being. Your responsibility is to be happy and to look for what is good for you and what is good for your family so that you can enjoy all the fruits of your business.

Analyze: Do you have any type of addiction? Is there anything that diverts you from what makes you thrive? What is it that makes you reach your maximum potential, or is there something that is stopping you and affecting your life?

You must find the answer and look for immediate solutions because it is a huge key to getting your business forward. If you have any type of addiction, change. All uncontrollable excesses can be called addiction, and this includes addiction to work excessively and constantly that does not allow you to have your balance and enjoy other areas that you deserve to enjoy.

Seek professional help if this is your case. Try to focus on how to enjoy the benefits that your business gives you. It's time to work on your passion, it's time to feel motivated, it's work time, and it shouldn't be affected by anything outside or your health.

One of my best recommendations for you is that you use the advantages of having your own business to give yourself some vacation time. Rest from your routine life, breathe as Trinidad breathed, and sit with your family and your friends, or alone, to enjoy your life. Be grateful for everything you have daily. Remember that life needs a balance, in which we do not overdo it anywhere, not even to work in a way that destroys health, family, and body. The body needs rest to focus again and recharge its batteries to continue fighting decisively. Meditating, reflecting, and planning are essential decisions that help you reach your maximum potential.

When I am working on helping entrepreneurs and business owners, I usually ask this question: "Why do you work independently?" and 80% usually answer things like: "Because I want to retire early," "because I want to have quality time with my family," or "because I want to be financially free." And what happens if we don't force ourselves to do it? Well, work will consume us, we will become addicted workers, stress will consume us, our tolerance will decrease due to being exhausted, and at any moment, our family can complain because they will feel that we prefer to work over them. The worst thing is that we will not realize it because we work so much and learn our craft to perfection; we are fascinated by doing it over and over again without any rest. Then the routine absorbs us, and the result is that we age at work, our features change, and it becomes a vice and an obsession.

Be grateful that you managed to have a job created by yourself, but when the time is right, learn to delegate, to have a business that moves on its own so that you can live and enjoy it, and thus, you can make your loved ones happier. Remember that they are a gift that God gave you. Enjoy your people.

Do this step intelligently; delegating is not done overnight. This requires the preparation of your new manager and your work team, the duplication of what you do in them, and the finding of the appropriate person to supervise your employees so that you have peace and can multiply your company's profits over and over again.

Remember that the objective of having your independent business is to have the freedom to balance your life and enjoy its advantages. You must learn to delegate and find a manager, not so that if you die sooner than expected, someone else will manage it, but so you can live your life now. Enjoy what is important to you because you want it, not because you have it. Take your business to be able to move on its own, even if you want to be there. He will be the vehicle through which you will grow and give your maximum potential for expansion.

I encourage you to grow as a business person, as a family person, as an example for your friends. Generate jobs for others and provide better income for your employees, and remember that your business has a giant purpose of prosperity not only for you but also for the people around you.

> *"If your wealth was easy to get, it will not*
> *be worth much to you."*
> **— Proverbs 20:21, ERV**

Reflect:

- What areas of your health do you need to work on?

_____

_____

- Are you having time for your health? Do you exercise?

_____

_____

- Are you visiting professionals to help you maintain your physical, mental, and spiritual health, and are you following their advice?

_____

_____

- Do you have healthy eating habits?

_____

_____

- Are you delegating so you can take time for yourself?

I encourage you to design a plan for your health and well-being, writing down the changes you are going to implement. For example, write down the time you will exercise, what eating plan you will follow, which professionals you will consult, and the regular visits you can schedule to monitor your progress. It also establishes prudent times for entertainment and rest to regain strength and start again. Remember that your health is your best partner.

Use Your Keys

O ur decisions build or destroy. Taking care of our heart, spirit, soul, and health with action and fighting laziness are the keys that open and close doors, allowing us to love ourselves and manage what is vital to undertake with quality of life. We are not machines; therefore, we must take care of the temple that runs the business that we want so much to be prosperous, and in difficult times, we must be patient and look for solutions so that our businesses do not fall. If we persevere through the most difficult times, the good times will be like a fantastic adventure in which we will reap all the benefits for which we have fought so hard.

It is very important to remain firm in faith, guarding our hearts, even from our thoughts, encouraging ourselves, and deflecting the negativity that may arrive at some point.

Our thoughts have a lot to do with our success or failure. The winning mentality added to faith will become a trustworthy tool to be successful and a great advantage to undertake. Using our faith to have the right mindset will defeat all our fears.

Genesis 1:28, (KJV)

"And God blessed them, and God said unto them, "Be fruitful and multiply, and replenish the earth, and subdue it; and have dominion over the fish of the sea, and over the fowl of the air, and over every living thing that moveth upon the earth."

The Lord specifically commanded us to be fruitful and multiply. So the meaning is clear: God wants families to grow and for more people to share his blessings and the gifts he gave us. He wants us to use our talents and prosper financially and spiritually. So, if that is our winning mentality, we will live with a purpose that will give us reasons to fight every day.

Let's not feel afraid. It's okay to be financially stable, have everything paid for, have no debt, grow as much as we can, and provide and educate our families to the best of our ability with a prosperous mindset. Let's cut the chains that take away so many blessings from us. Let's live the adventures that we want to fill our souls. Whatever our age, every minute of our life counts to turn on that light in our spirit. All these efforts are not only for us but also for a better future for everyone who crosses our path.

Most successful people who believe in God know that He wants what is best for them and will always be there to protect them. The secret is the state mentality of someone who knows that everything will be fine.

Part Four:
A Door to the Future

TWELVE

INNER GROWTH = FINANCIAL GROWTH

When we strengthen the spirit, soul, and health, we strengthen the foundations to achieve success in our purposes. If we can gradually combine each of these areas and understand that everything is a set of strengths for ourselves, being well, following advice, and learning from other people's experiences will be easier.

Let's get to know another story of power:

Melissa was experiencing beautiful spiritual growth, and her purpose in life was firm: she wanted to help everyone: her family, her friends, and even strangers. It was a very noble purpose, but she didn't realize that most of the time, she put everyone before herself. She went out of her way to meet the needs of others, leaving his own in a secondary place.

She worked in an office training and covering what the staff couldn't cover. Her relationship with clients was excellent, and she always made them feel that her company was willing to help. She liked her job so much that, on many occasions, she preferred to do things herself rather than delegate.

Melissa never worried about analyzing the type of friendships she had because she felt that she was strong enough not to be influenced by others. However, there came a time in her life when she realized what not choosing the people around her was doing to her: She received insults, she had "friendships" that were only with her out of convenience, she didn't have anyone when sick, she experienced other people's dramas, and she was involved in misunderstandings with unfair, envious people with bad intentions. Then, she understood that relating to people of good spirit was important, and she decided, after many disappointments, to change the way she selected the people around her. Since then, her health and spirit began to improve, her dreams began to revive, and she discovered that, with the help of the right people, she could progress further and take the company to another level.

Melissa understood that her time was valuable. She had a family, home, and work routine and made time for her responsibilities and dreams, but she didn't worry much about resting or focusing on herself or her inner growth. But she set out to make changes, and her life began to be more productive and happier. It was not easy because her personality always sought the well-being of others, which is not a bad thing, but she learned to identify what disturbed her inner peace and when it was time to move away to achieve harmony and avoid emotional exhaustion. She knew that growing spiritually could directly impact her financial growth.

Choosing where you focus your mind and time is essential to have peace of mind and focus on what you do well.

> *"Keep thy heart with all diligence, for out of it are the outflowings of life."*
> — *Proverbs 4:23. KJ21*

Melissa knew that thoughts before going to bed were very important to keep the heart and stay positive. For her, praying was considerably important; however, she did not do it every day, so when she began to do it constantly, she was able to rest better because she felt protected and safer.

Much later, she was able to have her family at a different stage with a better spiritual focus and better relationships, following steps of positivism and a healthy mind. Her main focus now was her mental health and protecting her heart. With the passage of time and the change of friends around her, her life improved spiritually, and her feelings of peace were different.

To have good finances and real prosperity, you need to seek spiritual peace. Watch where you put your thoughts and who you invest your energy in.

Don't Let the Past Damage the Harvest of the Present

Sandra was a fun and enthusiastic girl. She loved to pretend she could fly, and with her sisters, she dreamed of what they would be when they grew up. However, she did not feel loved. She lived in her little world, watching the children do different things, while she stayed at home with a frequently crying mother, a woman without many purposes beyond raising her daughters.

Sandra's father was a political leader in charge of many employees, admired and praised by everyone around him. He was always well fed, dressed, and perfumed from head to toe, as his wife took care of it. That woman gave her life for him while he put neighbors, family, and friends before her most of the time. He even made his flirtatious and elegant secretary a priority on some occasions, with whom he had a secret relationship for many years.

That was the environment in which Sandra grew up: overprotected on some occasions and ignored on many others in a dysfunctional family that fought in silence, without words, in loneliness, in contempt and rudeness, in looks without love, with the emptiness of a father who did not come home and a mother dying while still alive, who was rarely seen smiling. Sandra, unlike her sisters, did believe her mother's real sadness; she did not see her attitude as manipulation or rebellion because when no one saw her, almost kneeling at the entrance to her mother's room, Sandra watched her cry while her sisters slept. She saw how she was waiting for a husband who did not come home because he was drinking with friends.

Sandra felt like she was in a cage, a scared bird, alone, misunderstood by the world, and seen by her acquaintances as a weak, extremely sensitive, and ridiculous person. She was afraid all the time, like a little bird in a cage in the middle of a jungle with a lot of darkness.

But she decided to get out of that cage and grew up with the mentality that she did not want that life for herself, and she used all those reasons to get ahead, to not depend on anyone, not to have to borrow money, and that they could never treat her the way they treated her mother. Sandra fought to work hard and tirelessly so that no man or person would treat her like that. Although people saw Sandra as if she worked because she liked money, few understood that what motivated her was the spiritual strength not to let herself fall, not to see herself with depression like her mother, and not to see herself locked up and humiliated. Sandra worked to take her mind off her worries and feel useful and happy; she worked because she loved what she did and wanted financial freedom.

What began as a form of personal growth became a distraction to avoid the suffering of the loss of her parents, the divorce of her husband, and the betrayals of friends and loved ones.

Sandra knew that she had to occupy her mind with something with purpose, and she began to grow with successful businesses, generating jobs and helping others grow theirs. She looked for a way to have a purpose in life, to be happy doing what she likes. She learned to delegate, and that gave her more freedom to help others. Those who misunderstood that it was for money later understood that she worked for other reasons but that the money came in abundance because their purpose of doing the right thing was stronger.

When Sandra came out of her cage, she wanted to fly, to fulfill her dreams, to no longer be controlled, humiliated, and not understood. She was afraid of falling into her mother's life, to whom, no matter how much she tried, fought, and insisted, she could never help until her death because she had decided to stay in her emotional cage. After going to several psychologists, she understood that each person, including her, has the freedom to do what they want with their life and that we have to respect that decision, for better or worse. Then, she was able to rest and let go of her pain after a long time.

Despite her battles, Sandra used all that frustration to help people who did want to get ahead and did not let herself fall into depression, although on many occasions, she felt she was on the verge of one. She had good friendships and a lot of success at work, but after so many losses of family, significant others, friends, and family absence, she was on the verge of letting her life fall many times, but she held on to her purpose.

She held onto the truth that even though the world could fail her if she had God, she had everything.

At that moment, her whole life changed. She began to give more importance to healthy relationships, and she met a wonderful being who accompanied her, supported her, loved her, and had a beautiful son who filled her with life and purpose. Today, she feels proud of having been able to continue with her business and her life in times of tribulation. Life has taken a complete turn for her, and despite all her work benefits, economic stability, and not needing to work, she can live her entire life with what she has achieved. She knows that she is committed to sharing what she knows. She wants to help others, and her spirit feels grateful, lucky, and motivated to live happily in tribulations. She understands that life is not perfect, but every situation has a positive side that she always prefers to choose because she is the only one responsible for her happiness.

Now, instead of feeling like a caged bird, she feels like a butterfly that is constantly changing for the better. She knows she is not perfect, but she works on herself to enjoy her life instead of being in a jungle, in a beautiful forest full of flowers and spaces to know, explore, and enjoy. Now, she loves creating businesses with others, motivating and seeing others progress, enjoying what they have created with their families, finding happiness in seeing others happy, and seeing how they organize their finances and how their lives change. Sandra not only overcame herself, but she was able to do so by not letting her past affect her future.

As we can see, life is not easy; there are many stones in the way. However, success lies precisely in how these problems are handled, changing our point of view to one that benefits us mentally, spiritually, and physically.

Everyone lives their life the way they want to live it, and that must be respected. We cannot carry emotional burdens because of how the people we love live, even if they are our family members. It is a spiritual war that is difficult to fight but not impossible to win.

Do not let yourself down! Find a way to entertain your mind with something positive. It is not easy, but it is possible. If you need it, seek help; don't fight alone. Use your past as a platform that drives you to achieve your goals and dreams, and above all, do not let the seed of the past damage the harvest of the present.

> *"Whoever works his land will have plenty of bread, but he who follows worthless pursuits lacks sense."*
>
> **— Proverbs 12:11, ESV**

Reflect:

- Spiritually, are you growing every day?

- Are you overcoming your weaknesses, frustrations, and personality issues that affect how you feel?

- What new actions should you take to take care of your heart?

- Do you think that having a good spirit and a healthy soul can help you move your business forward faster?

- Are you finding the balance you wanted to have when you started your company? Are your "whys" motivating you to continue?

- Are you setting aside time to enjoy what makes you happy apart from work, family, and responsibilities?

Chapter
THIRTEEN
THE POWER
OF HEALTHY
RELATIONSHIPS

As we have seen throughout this book and reaffirmed in the previous chapter with Melissa's story, the people we interact with constitute a large part of who we are, and therefore, they have a great power to influence the success of our lives. When I talk about relationships, I am not only referring to those of a personal nature but also to all those that make up the relational circle of our business, that is, employees, clients, and suppliers, among others, with whom it is necessary to have healthy relationships that stimulate our growth.

Your business is a gift from God, but if God gives you something and you don't work on it or value it, you will most likely lose it. That's the same thing that happens with relationships; if you don't work on them, you can lose them.

I give you several examples of common thoughts that make relationships fail:

- "I will treat my spouse in any way I want, and I will relax because, in the end, what has to happen will happen."

- "God is in control of my business, and it will prosper no matter how I treat my employees."

- "What belongs to you, no one takes away from you. I don't have to try harder." (With this mentality, you can lose business and referrals..)

We need to learn to respect everyone because if we do not do so, we may inadequately serve a customer and even affect a sale because we could not put ourselves in their shoes and could not understand their needs. We have free will, and our actions have fruits or consequences in our relationships. If a client is not appreciated and is not treated concerning their needs, they can go somewhere else where they will be listened to.

On many occasions, the mind leads us to treat someone who reminds us of another person who caused us harm in the past, and we act unfairly for that person, for our business, and for us, who, in addition to going through those situations that affected us in the past, now we have to pay such a high price.

It is also important to know that when we deposit wisdom, help, dedication, and service, and the vessel is not good, the fruits will not be for a good job.

Business is an art with which you help others with your products, but you have to listen carefully to the needs of the consumer. Not everything is for everyone, and if someone doesn't want, appreciate, or value what you are giving, you will gain more if you can let it go in peace since there are always clients or future clients who will happily and gratefully value what you provide. Not everyone is going to see your business the same way, and that's okay, so let the next one come with peace, and may the previous one live in harmony. The important thing is to be aware that you tried to provide an excellent service, because if you didn't and apart from that you get angry because the client doesn't want to work with you, then you won't grow, and on the contrary, you will be filled with frustration by not understanding why people don't want to work with you.

Trying to see the other person's problems from a different perspective will also make you feel good, knowing that you have done the best you can do. This will help you not have regrets and sleep peacefully every time your day ends.

When faced with conflicts, the best thing to do is to provide solutions, providing ideas on how things can be done. If criticism is constructive, it is appreciated and analyzed if it fits with someone else's ideals before taking action. Talking with solutions motivates you to have good relationships with clients or critics, and this peaceful attitude improves you. Whether there is a problem or not, the key is how to resolve any situation quickly and on good terms.

This is a very important issue because if, as an entrepreneur, you do not build the ability to solve, the dynamics of progress are delayed, and those small obstacles can turn into big ones just because you have not taken an effective step of action from the beginning. The most effective people can bring solutions quickly; if you don't, the mission fades, the quality deteriorates, and you can leave loose threads that can affect your business. It is important to always take immediate action so as not to let any problem progress beyond what is necessary.

Each experience makes us better and helps your clients, but supporting your team is also necessary to start having quality. Teaching your collaborators to do things in a better way, to overcome mistakes, and to explain the consequences of their actions is the same as training your work team with the same mission and ethics that you have. These are actions that protect the company and the customer at the same time.

So that a conflict does not repeat itself, we must find as many solutions as possible. For many, it is frustrating to work with people who do not want to help or who are incompetent at their job because it is like a hard wall that you cannot break through. We are not perfect, but the desire to help solve problems is a giant advantage for the progress of a business. In that case, it is better to find someone who wants to help you both as an employee and when you are a client so as not to suffer the loss of time and stress that stops your business. Start working on your team.

Depending on the type of company you have, you may or may not require staff, and in both cases, there are advantages and disadvantages. Being the sole owner of a company has the advantages of not depending on the decisions of others and not needing as much capital for salaries when starting. I advise you that if you can be the sole owner of your company, whether large or small, you can do it without partners so that you avoid many headaches since we are all different. This way, you avoid having to consult for decisions, which gives you peace and tranquility.

With this, I am not saying that it is bad to have a partner if you feel that you cannot do it alone because having someone by your side who complies with the company's ethics can be wonderful. What I want to tell you is to be careful and choose your entrepreneurial partner very well because a partnership is like a marriage with children, where the baby is the business. Therefore, the decision about who you partner with is vital since it takes a lot of time to build it, and you don't want to end up frustrated by a bad decision, realizing years later that you wasted all that time.

I recommend that, if you decide to take on a partner, even if it is a family member or a friend, you do an in-depth interview and give yourself the time to get to know them in the business field to see how they work, even to ask for references and see what their credit history is. Find a responsible person, and remember that you would not give your baby just any father or mother. Choose carefully and make decisions with too much analysis to avoid failure in the future that will steal your peace, which is priceless.

On the other hand, you must keep in mind that to grow, you need to delegate. When a business starts to grow rapidly, if you don't seek help, you stagnate and can become frustrated that you can't be alone. It has happened to many entrepreneurs that they have ended up wanting to close just because they do not have enough staff.

This decision also depends on your goals and why you have your business. If your purpose, for example, is to have more time for your family and travel, you will most likely have to delegate. A team is also important if you want to ensure that your businesses can manage themselves and you can have business chains. To grow, seeking support is essential.

Clarity in Relationships

The key to feeling proud of good service is clarity with your client, explaining in detail how your product is handled, if possible, in writing.

Many businesses are lost due to a lack of clarity and fear that things will not be fulfilled as promised. Mutual agreement deals are essential, and this includes dates, places, and a good definition of what is expected, with solutions in the best and worst situations. Yes, verbal deals can be fulfilled, and you trust your client, but you can also have unknown clients, and if you do not have credibility with them, a sale is difficult to happen.

Please read this very carefully: many legal problems begin, and many couples, families, and friendships are lost due to lack of clarity. And if this happens with loved ones and close people, imagine what would happen with another human being that you don't even know.

Read Carlos's story:

Carlos was a great businessman, very organized and honest, who constantly trained and provided good training for his team so as not to make mistakes. He was good at his finances, and this always kept him motivated to dream big.

However, despite doing his job to the best of his ability, he had a situation that caused a client to want to sue him. Carlos was very surprised because he knew that he had been clear with that client, that everything had been explained to him, verbally and in writing, many times, that there were many notes, many emails, always trying to help him, exceeding the service, and explaining pros and cons of his products.

Documents were sent from all the communications that demonstrated that everything was correct before the law, documented, and well organized, and the court dismissed the case. Although the story ended well, as the client apologized, acknowledged the mistake, and dropped the lawsuit, it was very stressful for Carlos to feel the injustice. However, when he remembered in those moments of anguish and fear what could happen and that God fought for him as he fought for his own, he felt faith, and this not only brought him peace but a miracle caused a change in the heart of his client, which led him to do the right thing and continue maintaining a good business relationship.

Carlos was not only able to present documentation that he had done the right thing, but he was also able to see God's blessing, not only for the support in a situation that wanted to steal his peace but also for the fact of having a fruitful business that would have allowed him to pay a lawyer, it would have needed. Therefore, having documentation is important, having faith and seeing the benefits of how a company can satisfy many needs.

Working for yourself has many advantages, but you have to be extremely organized to prevent misunderstandings and be able to have legal evidence that everything was done correctly and in the best way, with good faith.

It is not appropriate for people to be confused, but it is common. A client can forget what was promised, and this can bring frustrations and problems for everyone, contributing to losing motivation due to excess problems and misunderstandings. Keeping everything in order is the construction of good habits that perhaps represent a sacrifice of several days in exchange for peace, harmony, and success. Taking the time to clarify documents, services, advantages, and disadvantages is essential.

People need clarity in detail. This increases communication and efficiency and prevents frustration for either party.

Concerning employees, you need clarity in assignments, clarity in how things have to be done, clarity in how many hours you should work, clarity in when and how you should be paid, and clarity in how the systems and the necessary equipment work, and how to handle it to prevent damage. If this is missing, it will cause frustration in the people who help you in your company, ultimately affecting the entire business.

Gratitude and support for your employees with a good attitude is essential. The people who are working with you must feel that they can count on you, and that will make you feel that you can count on them. You set the limits and responsibilities, but if you want to count on your team, they must understand, feel, and receive the support of their leader.

Remember that not everyone has the same point of view, nor does everyone have the same opinion about every issue, every problem, or fear that arises. For every situation, there is no single answer. There are usually many ways to solve something. That is why it is good not to assume, and that is why good dialogue is so important in business. You reach common terms in contracts, you listen to the opinions of both parties, and you reach an agreement in which everyone is okay. Be clear about what you do, and you will be able to continue on your path without fear.

Now, know Teresa's story:

Teresa was a business owner, but she was sad, frustrated, and full of doubts because there was an employee in her business who caused her anxiety and instability. She did not feel calm because of the accumulation of errors on the part of her employee and because of the impudence and abuse with which she faced it. The problem is that Teresa was not able to let her go; she was afraid of doing so, and therefore, she lost more employees. She knew that she had to make a decision and choose better people for her business since most of them, although they were not suitable, had been hired for fear of not getting good employees for her business.

She was finding it extremely difficult to get ahead, she was afraid to grow her business so as not to be left alone, she felt trapped in her business, she did the work half-heartedly, she faced many cancellations in her sales, and she discovered that her employees told her that they did the work and not they did it. Then she met an employee recruitment company, and they found the right person.

One of the biggest mistakes in business is losing clarity and not having the confidence to, as an employer, tell someone to work in a specific way at the company and express what they do well and what they need to work on. If a correction is not made in time, you cannot expect the person in the company to do it well. If they're not doing it right and have no guidance, it wouldn't be their fault. Always remember that employees are your image; it is how you multiply and extend yourself through them. That is why it is necessary that you invest a lot of time in training and preparing the people who are in your company; that says a lot about you. Having employees is having the ability to work for them. We will talk about that in more depth in the next chapter.

If you have a product that covers your investment when you sell it, you have the profits you need to keep it afloat. However, the focus of your business should not be on money but on people, taking care of fulfilling your responsibilities well so that once you establish fair prices for your business and the client, you can dedicate yourself to offering what helps. As I mentioned before, don't worry, the money will come by itself if all the keys provided are used the right way to open the doors given.

The most prosperous businesses are the businesses that only require service, such as real estate, insurance, taxes, advice, etc., because the investment you are putting in is minimal and depends more on who you are, on how you treat the client, on how you solve the client when they have a problem. The primary focus is on goals, who you are, and how the company and employees are run. That shows the power of good relationships.

> "It is better to eat a little where there is love than to eat a lot where there is hate."
> — **Proverbs 15:17, ERV**

Love and Financial Progress

A Story of Power

This is the story of Raquel, an entrepreneur, fair, intelligent woman with great ideas in business, full of life, and with a lot of faith. She had several businesses that allowed her to work only if she wanted, and she had good financial stability, but she made very bad decisions in love. It was incredible how she could be so intelligent in some aspects of her life and, in others, a total failure. Even though they were two very different personal areas of her life, these obstacles of not making good personal decisions were affecting her emotional state and hindering progress in her business with peace. Her decisions were causing her spirit to die little by little.

One day, Raquel meets a very kind boy, a total gentleman, and someone very friendly. Raquel, with so much accumulation of disappointments, initially finds a good friendship in him. After many beautiful moments, memories of love, and approximately two years, they decide to live together. After

15 days of doing it, her gallant and chivalrous lover changed completely. Raquel began to have obstacles in her progress because she did not make good decisions.

Raquel's story is one of those that happens every day to many people who want to improve themselves and manage to get ahead during difficulties, but it was very difficult for Raquel to see how living in the midst of it affected a human due to the abuse. As everything progressed little by little, she did not understand why her desire to build her business was disappearing at the same time.

She felt sad because of her partner's unfair and untrue accusations, and in a moment of desperation, and this time without planning it and without knowing that Raquel would go through this, her partner one day became someone she no longer recognized. He became more and more of a verbal and physical abuser, and he was almost on the verge of killing her. The last day she was with him, he threw her at the walls of the room; he was very strong, and she was very afraid. He took her away. He locked her in the room and frightened her, saying that he was going to burn the house down with her inside, that no one would notice it, that neither her family nor anyone cared about her, that her business was not worth it, and he also mentioned that she would never achieve her ridiculous dreams.

Raquel was a happy person, but she was bothered by injustices and false accusations. She only heard degrading words as if they were coming from the enemy to defeat a giant and a wonderful purpose that God had for her. He kept turning off her light and repeated as many degrading words as he could. She just closed her eyes and repeated to herself, "That is not true. It is the enemy that wants to destroy me and is not going to achieve it. I can do everything he is telling me I can't; I have demonstrated it." She repeated to herself: "That is not true, he is lying."

In the middle of the nightmare and the story as a horror movie, he mercilessly decided to push her aggressively and then choke her by the neck, and she, lying on the ground without being able to breathe, could feel death. She thought that was the last day of her life, and she began to pray to our Father inside her, and she did not put up any more resistance. She saw in his eyes a monster, someone she had never seen, as big as if he were profound evil as if he was not even him. She continued praying, and when she gave up and thought it was the end, as if by some miracle, he had given it up. He calmed down completely, and he changed his face as if ashamed. It was on the second floor, and the kitchen was downstairs. He left the room, and when he left, she found the keys on the floor that he dropped. She was able to quickly go down the stairs, thinking that he was no longer there, but she saw him sitting almost at the end of the stairs, seated as if exhausted and with a giant knife at his side. Like another miracle, she did not know from where, from one moment to the next, an inexplicable peace began. Everything was so calm for both of them, in a situation like that, she told him: "Calm down, calm down, I know it wasn't you. You wouldn't be able to do that. Tomorrow will be a better day to talk." She promised him that she wouldn't call the police so that he wouldn't get upset and do something to her. She told him very calmly, but inside, she was full of fear and she continued praying. She told him, "I'm going to take the knife slowly, and I'm going to put it in the kitchen."

She had no idea the peace with which she spoke to him, and inside, she was exploding in fear. When she went to the kitchen, which was located near the garage door, to leave the house, she left the knife and ran to her car. He was blocking her with his car, but she finally managed to back up a little, got on top of the grass, and was able to get out quickly. There, her spirit was further destroyed, not only by losing the person who she believed would never do that to her but because she felt that she couldn't take it anymore. She cried until she couldn't anymore.

Never in her life did she imagine that she would have this obstacle to move forward, to have a healthy family, that she would go through this, but she was able to recognize that moment that she could not do it alone and that she had to get out of this situation, no matter what the cost.

For this reason, she lost days of work while she recovered. It helped her to have employees who could cover her obligations at the time, thanks to the fact that she was the owner, but this warrior was labeled as weak due to her kindness, trust, and love for others.

Without having energy and with a lot of pain from having allowed this to happen to her, she sought help; she went to domestic violence groups and met many women who went through even worse situations for not making good decisions in love or many who put up with many things out of financial need, not having money or work to get ahead on their own, and they did not prepare for emergencies like these. Many women there had been unable to get out of something so toxic for years and years, and now they were looking for help because they were in situations with obstacles to moving forward and progressing with peace and harmony.

Initially, out of fear, she stayed with relatives, but then, thanks to the fact that she already had her business, a way to have a constant income, she was able to move and pay for a place to be able to live alone in an environment of no violence. She was able to do it, so being financially well and having flexibility in her business allowed her to keep progressing despite the problems. Yes, while she was recovering, she had to increase her employees' hours in the office so as not to lose clients and so that they would be happy, but she managed to ensure that neither the staff nor the clients in the office realized what was happening to protect her business and not mix the personal with the work. The main key was to get out of the situation quickly, endure the pain she had to endure, heal, and move on.

She always saw work as a distraction since she was doing what she loved, and with those financial blessings from God, she was able to pay for the therapy and start again from the beginning in a different place emotionally. It took her a lot of effort to heal, but she did it, and this obstacle did not stop her progress. That is why I want to tell you that it is good to have financial stability and not let a person destroy us because we are not prepared. She thought that God helped her because He saw all her efforts and everything she always did to not let herself fall. Being grateful and never angry with God for her moments of weakness and problems, she felt the conviction that her financial prosperity also came from Him for a special purpose.

I am sure that God wants to bless you in every way, and you are here for a reason. Raquel now feels proud, even though, at some point, she felt ashamed for living like this because she dreamed of having a harmonious home. This situation was causing her to slowly lose a feeling of purpose in this life.

But she didn't stay there; she was able to admirably get up, even if she felt a lot of emotional pain doing so. The most important thing is that she sought help; she is not dead, as she didn't allow that situation to continue. He had faith and determination. She worked to replenish her spirit and is now a wonderful woman who pushes others to move their businesses forward during these types of circumstances.

I tell you this story not to scare you but to help you see a reality that many people go through and do not prosper, and also to see one example among many of how a bad decision in love and something so personal also affects your progress.

Raquel remained positive but did not make wise decisions in love, and allowing this event had consequences for her health and, therefore, for her business. She felt very grateful to be alive, but this caused her to have physical situations as a result. After this terrible event, she wanted to wait for her neck to stop hurting, and after waiting many years with these discomforts, they had to do two implants in her neck. A scar will be on her neck every day as a consequence, but she felt grateful for having that business, which gave her so many blessings.

The story did not end there. Thanks to her business, which continued running when she could not get out of bed and amid obstacles, the company continued well, the employees continued well, and she continued receiving income from her business while she recovered.

I insist on this story so that you see that beyond money. Being financially well helps you overcome difficulties over which you have no control. Years later, Raquel continued to multiply her businesses with peace and family support, making better decisions in love and her business.

Many years have passed, and Raquel today sees the difference in having a partner who shows her peace and love. Even though she and her current partner are not perfect, she is living with someone without violence of any kind. She discovered that this is priceless, and it is possible to feel the difference between a home of peace and harmony. For her, having a healthy partner was a huge change. Her progress was greater, and later, she had a beautiful son. She discovered that living with a person with a good temperament makes it easier to have motivation, and you enjoy success more with someone who wants you to progress.

I'll tell you something my friend read to me: It is easier to carry out a business when you have problems if you surround yourself with positive people who know how to solve problems calmly and effectively.

In conclusion, for Raquel, having a business amid obstacles helped her get ahead without having to depend financially on someone, to continue supporting her business during problems, to solve part of her health expenses, and to support herself while she was in bed until her full recovery.

Before continuing, I want to make a brief parenthesis to tell you that if you are in an abusive relationship, you need to seek professional help and get out of there immediately. Don't be afraid; don't let that paralyze you. There are support groups that will help you find a solution and a path to a new opportunity. You deserve more than what you are experiencing, and you can't wait until it's too late.

> *"The blessings of the LORD maketh rich,*
> *and He addeth no sorrow with it."*
> **— Proverbs 10:22, KJ21**

Reflect:

- Do you think that a business without a mentality of benefiting others will be able to multiply?

_____

_____

- Are you doing the best you can in your relationships? How is your treatment of others?

_____

_____

- Have you decided to stay away from toxic people?

_____

_____

- Are you cultivating healthy relationships?

_____

_____

- Do your relationships help or hurt your business?

_____

_____

- What areas do you need to work on to have healthier relationships?

  _____

  _____

- How do your customers and employees perceive you? Do they trust you or fear you?

  _____

  _____

Chapter
FOURTEEN
THE KEY TO GOOD TRAINING.

Training for your team is vital!!

No matter how much experience someone has, we are all different, including you, as owner of your company. It is impossible for your workers to be fortune tellers and to know your ideas and preferences if you are not communicating them to them. Good communication is essential if you want to save frustration: yours and your team's. Your employees don't want to feel frustrated and disoriented, as this causes instability and insecurity. People need to feel comfortable and confident in what they do, or they will start to doubt, and at the end of the day, that doubt will hurt your company.

Your team should be a representation of what YOU would do and what THEY would do, just like you if you were NOT present.

As leaders, we must ensure that we not only prepare ourselves, enhancing our innate talents, but also that we provide the right information to the team. In fact, before starting training, you should have a meeting to know If the new workers agree with the way the company is handled and if they are willing to execute that training.

Depending on your type of business, you must train them and obtain appropriate licenses for its development and compliance, including regulations that specify what is mandatory and what is not. Make sure that your licenses and paperwork remain current for as long as you work for your company.

After this initial training, once they have started working, a second training is recommended for the next ninety days. After that time, it is recommended that more training be provided in the workplace every week. This is one recommendation based on the amount of training your company needs. If this is extended, you will be more likely to do your job better. It is normal that at first they only tend to retain around 30% of what they have learned and that, due to the nerves and anxiety of doing it well, they do not practice correctly what they are taught, so it is important to review with them frequently in the first three months. All of this is added to the weekly training sessions and small daily or regular meetings, which also help keep the work team motivated and allow any pending doubts to be resolved.

Something that is also crucial during training is giving them instructions on how to answer the phone. The greeting is essential for the company's image, so it is good for your work team to memorize word by word the greeting you want them to use. For example: "Thank you for calling (company name). It is a pleasure to serve you today. How can I help you?"

It is also necessary to teach how to respond if they ask about someone who is not there or if the person being asked about is helping another customer. It is important to create a system where there is always someone who can help the client at the moment since depending on only one person knowing how to solve something puts you in a position of a problem if that person cannot be there. For example: "(Name) is helping someone else/outside the office, but I'd be happy to help."

For this, it must be taken into account that there are services that require an exclusive person for the benefit of the client or not to harm a sale already made, so it is good to look for a fair compensation system for the entire team that motivates them to want to help each other and help customers.

Additionally, it is advisable to train staff on how to handle situations when there are many phone calls at the same time, emphasizing the importance of not missing calls, regardless of whether they are many or few because your business depends on them. Some companies use techniques like these:

- The first example is with occasional call volume where many employees are not needed at the company, as there is enough time to help all customers. In this situation, the person in charge quickly captures all phone calls and puts the customer on hold, explaining that you are helping someone else in the line, giving you the option of calling them back as soon as the other call ends, or waiting on the line, if they prefer.

- Example: "I will be happy to assist you as soon as I finish helping this customer. Is it okay with you? I will be sure to help you with everything you need as soon as possible."

- In other cases, for example, in a solar panel presentation, roofing, or products where the family set aside a specific time, focus and answering extensive questions are required. My recommendation is that in cases of scheduled presentations that you know in advance will take time, you should not receive other calls since your clients need your full attention. Here, we are not talking about a *call center* but about people who allocate time for you, and if you don't have it, you will lose their attention.

- Another option that other companies are leaning toward is that in their message, they give an estimated time for when calls will be returned. This is especially used by consulting businesses, in the health branch, or similar, where the person being called may be attending to a patient or client for one or two hours, and they can't answer.

In all cases, whenever serving a client, the person must maintain a good attitude, be motivated, happy, smiling—even on the phone—and have a desire to serve. This will not only improve the day of those who practice it but also transfer the desire to buy. On the contrary, bad attitudes make people say no.

Transfer happiness, and your sales will increase.

Management systems

Organization is vital in any company, and for this, it is necessary to find a management system that fits your type of business, be useful to save all the applications and sales made, as well as the reports of any documentation that covers the company and clients.

As part of employee training, they should be given clear instructions, in detail and in writing, on how to handle said management systems. I recommend creating a document that specifies how to create a client if it has not yet been generated, what data should be included (name, last name, reference, contact information...), how to change data, add information, etc. If it is a type of business where a customer has more than one product, create a folder with documents. If the information is organized well and your clients allow it, everything you reflect in the system can serve as a database to promote your other products or future activities.

It is also very important, especially in the professions that require licenses, such as insurance or real estate, to find methods for clients to sign electronically. This is extremely beneficial because it saves paper, saves time, multiplies effectiveness, and increases clarity with the client since it allows them to take the time needed to read before signing.

Each step, no matter how simple or basic, must be explained in detail in said document, and you must demand that the team ensure that absolutely all information is reflected in the system. Training is essential to form a good team, especially when it comes to technology or management of personal and relevant information since there are people who, by fear of making mistakes or fear of technology, decide to write on paper to later insert it into the system, which is double the work with a great risk of information being lost.

Another recommendation I make is that you require that every request made by a client be requested in writing. With this, you prevent the client from saying that he did not request it, even if it is due to an oversight without bad intention. Once this request is received, you or your employees must go to the company's website or management system and reflect on the change in the client's file. Remember that good relationships are in clarity.

Keep in mind that options and time should always be given to make changes and help people. Sometimes, the customer has "buyer's remorse." However, if you answer all the questions they have as many times as they need you, or if they ask you to change something, make an effort to change it and enjoy the satisfaction of pleasing your clients. Just meeting their needs and overcoming their fears will make a client extremely happy and even willing to refer people. Train your team for those situations.

Another important aspect of management systems is reminders. Explain to your team how to save them in the system and what are the times to complete the tasks depending on the objective and requirements of your business. Be realistic in these assignments because, depending on the type of company and services offered, there may be projects that last months.

A good assignment may seem tedious because it contains many steps, but the reality is that once it is designed, it makes it easier to carry out tasks that may seem simple to you but are not simple for someone just starting. Keep in mind that when someone doesn't know that step that is basic to you, they can become frustrated and waste half an hour on something that takes minutes to do.

Workers must have clear references so they do not have to depend on others who want or do not want to help them. For example:

1. Click on the folder on the left.

2. Create the client, go to the pen, and select options.

3. Place the action with the solution, select the check mark, check, date, and save.

4. Make sure the notes are under the corresponding client so that all colleagues can see them.

5. Set today's date to solve it.

6. Save.

Regulations Regarding Employees

In your training, there are other types of rules that you must specify to maintain clarity with your employees and avoid uncomfortable circumstances. For example:

- **Dress code:** Can you go in *jeans* to work? Will they have a uniform? Can they wear casual or professional attire? Why do you want that kind of presentation? Is this something your team would be comfortable with? Would it help the production?

- **Use of personal phones:** Decide if you will allow phones as part of your job requirements for personnel in the office or work area. Many companies don't have restrictions on personal phones, and that's fine. For other companies, it is very important to work with people who understand that phones are not allowed. As technology evolves, we become more addicted to it, to the point of affecting the job. Having a team member who wants to be on their phone more with his personal affairs than performing the tasks for which he has been hired is harmful. If this needs to be clarified, there may be frustrations on the part of the supervisor and the rest of the workers since a colleague does not finish his tasks. In the long run, it affects the rest of the team since responsibilities are loaded on the colleagues. Having personal cell phones in many companies not only harms the company but also the work environment. Therefore, these situations should be clear from training. Some companies put notes like this: "Personal cell phones are not allowed. Always keep your phone turned off, in your bag, or your car. Please feel free to give the office number to your family in case of an emergency."

- **Responsibilities**: In your training, you must be clear with the position that the people are going to occupy. Tell them what the job is and what they should do in that position. Ask them if they will need someone else and also if they would be flexible to cover other positions or tasks if necessary. People should be willing to help others if there is an emergency, especially supervisors or people in command positions. These types of employees make us feel more secure since they know a little about everything and can even go so far as to handle the entire company as managers. On the other hand, others respond with a "that's not what they hired me for," and if that was not made clear from the beginning, I'm sorry to tell you that even if you don't like it, they are right. Along with the functions, you must explain in what order the daily tasks should be performed and what their priority is. This will help with effective time management without having to make decisions stopping teamwork just because employees are waiting for answers.

- **Attitude:** Clarifies the importance of positivism and a good attitude. There is nothing worse than having someone complaining all the time. What is the best description of complaining? Talk about something without giving a solution. Problems are going to always exist, but talking to people who provide solutions is the best.

  Maintaining a negative attitude all the time is contagious for the rest of the team. This delays and, in many cases, takes away concentration. The important thing is to move the business forward and enjoy the process. Having people like this takes away the opportunity for others to motivate themselves daily, to work happily toward the objectives, and to help others so that they want to get to work. That is the environment that, for you as the owner of the business, is convenient for you to have. Even customers notice when there is joy at work. Questioning without providing solutions is negativity.

- **Payment:** Establish amounts and methods of payment for your team, indicating whether they will have a salary or commissions and what the conditions are to obtain them.

- **Schedules**: Make work and service hours very clear. This must also be clear to customers since there is nothing more frustrating for them than not knowing what schedules you can find the people they need. Explain how being late or missing work can affect the increase in salaries in the annual review, or it could make them lose their job. Explain how they should notify someone if they will be late or cannot go to work. Explain in writing what time your company requires if someone is absent so that another person can cover, including emergencies. Some jobs require supporting documents, and others do not; you have to check the regulations and know if they are appropriate according to the country or business agreement. Usually, in companies where there are many employees, medical documentation is requested to reduce excuses, even if it is about an emergency due to medical problems.

- **Vacation**: Establish vacation requests in advance so that the company can prepare them. Ask them to have authorization before making plans. All companies have their own needs and possibilities, but the important thing is to clarify them to prevent the frustration of all the parties and ensure that the company is not affected by a lack of responsibility. Some companies would not be affected because a member of the team is missing, so it does not matter if they are not there as long as they comply with the tasks. Also, clarify if the type of work has high seasons where vacations cannot be authorized.

- **Fire or Resign:** In your training, you should clarify how much notice an employee should give notice of their resignation, how much time is considered "open door" time if they decide to return or for you to be able to provide good references in their new job, and what criteria are grounds for dismissal. This is very necessary because before a customer is affected or vital information for the company is lost, sometimes it is necessary to remove a person immediately. Some companies ask that the person who is leaving give two or three weeks' notice to have time to train others before leaving. This, of course, will depend on the type of work and how trustworthy the departing team member has proven to be. To make this decision, it is important to ask yourself: is the company firing him, or does he want to leave? What were the reasons for that decision? Has he been loyal throughout his history as an employee of the company? Do you agree with any pre-prepared document, such as a non-compete or confidentiality agreement? What are your ethics concerning helping the client? If you decided to stay, would you put the company at risk? Make the rules regarding clients very clear: once a person stops working at your company, or even while there, the employee should not take clients to another location unless previously agreed. You don't want to work hard, paying salaries, marketing, and all the expenses that come with maintaining your business so that later things happen that you don't want to happen.

With issues of schedules, absences or delays, and vacations, it is very important to emphasize the necessity of planning since co-workers and the company itself are affected if they cannot be organized as a team. In the absence of a person, it can feel overwhelming, and this causes tension that ends up affecting business prosperity.

About Customers and Products

Personal Information:

Defending a client's privacy is essential for success. Neither you nor anyone on your team can share their information without their authorization under any circumstances. The client trusts you, and not protecting their data puts them at risk. Depending on the information, this client could be a victim of identity theft or something more delicate. Furthermore, in many countries, data protection is highly regulated, and committing an infraction of this type can result in very large fines. In addition to this, it must be added that it is unethical to distribute any type of information from someone who trusted you.

Processes:

- Make a detailed list of the documents required when a customer wants to obtain a product or contract service.

- Define what to do when your company cannot serve a client: Do they transfer them to another company? Under what limits or conditions?

Products or services:

- Clearly explain the scope of coverage for any type of product or service you offer. Make it clear what you include and what you don't, and that employees always know how to explain it to the customer before payment is made. People do not buy what they are not clear about; They give their money in exchange for something, so if there is no benefit for them, or areas that may be confusing are not clarified, it is rare that there are sales.

- In your training, clarify the steps to make a quote from your company. It is easy for a client to leave if they do not receive something clear and professional from the company that clarifies the benefit they will receive. Sometimes, the client believes that avoiding clarifications will increase the price. This does not give confidence. It is also important to emphasize the times for quoting since many people understand that if a quick estimate arrives, they will work in the same way. If it takes you a while to send a quote and another company's quote comes in faster or they send a quote at the same time as you, they expect a similar service and assume it will take longer, the same time, or less time to deliver your service. Today, there is a perception of greater professionalism, and you can lose the client. Check if there is an automatic system that allows you to solve this instantly or with more agility, and before sending an estimate, make sure the person involved double-checks all applicable discounts and presents options. Train your team to talk about the credibility of the company and look for a product that helps people. Cover your concerns to always help. Ask questions about what the customer needs, and never assume that he doesn't want your product. Listen, listen, listen! Ask for the information that you don't have. If your client does not want something you offer, the ideal is for them to let you know why so you can find solutions. Respond with solutions.

Ask yourself: what is the customer looking for? Listening, responding, and accommodating their needs in response is vital. If you don't cover them, it's difficult for them to want to get your product. Most of the time, just by asking the right questions, your sales increase and cover the needs of those you want to help.

- Train on how to give a realistic time expectation to clients. What is the average time it may take to provide a quote after receiving the customer information and then delivering a product? Does the client understand it? Are you clear? What is the average time necessary to perform a service per client for your company?

- You must also train your team very well on how to refute objections. Train with everything positive about the product and everything negative that may happen in a sale to be able to propose solutions. Your employees must reflect firmness and security, and it must be noted that they are well trained and that they do not have doubts or create confusion. This will happen easily if you can train them to know the products perfectly. Give yourself the gift of maintaining, for yourself and your team, the presentation in writing with the list of all your products, written word by word, identifying and highlighting the keywords or concepts that will be essential for said presentation. This will help you because nerves, inexperience, lack of practice, and even ego can play tricks at the time of a sale, and that's where customer frustrations come from.

Motivate yourself to be the first to learn the presentation and do it completely, in order, and do it one hundred percent of the time you explain a product. Once your presentation is approved and learned, you will no longer have to think so much; you will do it, and that's it. Simple! That way, you will enjoy your day-to-day life more.

- Explain in great detail how to receive payments, whether the system allows you to receive credit cards, cash, money orders, bank transfers, or any form of payment that allows you to accept. Not knowing this detail can damage a sale.

Talk Less, Act More

Why have a business owner or team member? Does talking too much affect your company's production?

While you talk, if it is not in the interest of a client, you waste the time that you should take advantage of to work and be productive. Also, someone who explains too much makes the customer tired, or they can be overwhelmed with so much information that they decide to come back another day because they need to think about it. Too much information is tiring; that's why it's better to listen carefully to what they ask for. This way, you will be more efficient, and you will have very satisfied customers.

Focus on the doubts and answer exactly what they ask you so that the client does not think that you are avoiding them with many explanations. Answering only "yes," "no," "mmmm," "uh-huh," or any other sound that is not clear to them and makes the expert seem complicated. As I said before, listening more has more benefits.

How can workers in your company work less and be more productive? Following instructions. It helps delight customers and offer what your company offers the way you want. Having all the questions answered when quoting your product helps employees not to have to waste time coming and going. Do your best from the beginning. Pay attention to the details.

Why is it so important to have staff who are excellent at following instructions? Because when you follow instructions, you do exactly what the customers want; you please them. Don't forget that we are here to help people and make them happy, as long as it does not affect the ethics of the company and the client. It becomes easier to train and help new members of the team to do better if they are good at following instructions.

Each step of training has a long-experienced reason time, in many cases. Therefore, if we want a company to be successful and we know that the formula has worked for them for a long time, we should respect it and learn the proven process.

Motivate the team; if your answer is negative to them, they won't feel supported. Please provide a solution in which the effectiveness has been demonstrated. If a person follows all the company's instructions and they do not work, it will be the company's fault, not the employee's. Therefore, it doesn't hurt to clarify it so that they can follow the training with confidence.

Ability to produce wealth -

"You may say to yourself, 'My power and the strength of my hands have produced this wealth for me.' [18] *But remember the LORD your God, for it is he who gives you the ability to produce wealth, and so confirms his covenant, which he swore to your ancestors, as it is today."*

— Deuteronomy 8:17-18, NIVUK

Reflect:

- What products or services do you want to offer?

_____

_____

- Do you know everything about your product or service?

_____

_____

Dare to write a training manual!

We all have that capacity, believe it! But without action, spirit, or motivation, how are you going to achieve it? Apart from good, conscious, and common-sense training, you can motivate them so that they enjoy working for you. Make a plan with each of your goals as well. The most important thing about what you see on paper and what you don't see anywhere is to find the clarity that gives confidence. Without a good plan, plus not having in mind the spiritual guide that fills you with a lot of hope and faith, it can become impossible for many to carry out such great purposes. Remember to make your plan fun so that you enjoy having a good working team for your benefit and also theirs.

Chapter FIFTEEN

DREAM AGAIN AND WORK ON YOUR FINANCES

Financial problems affect us all at some point in our lives, but it is never too late to get ahead. We have financial problems not because of a lack of management capacity but because we lack organization, action, and good guidance. Sometimes, we do not have adequate information because we have not been taught to manage our money or we have not been taught to manage one of the best sources, which is the Word of God.

In this chapter, I will share with you a support plan and a lot of material to help you achieve balance in your economy. It is a very practical chapter, so you will find many reflection questions that I encourage you to answer to make it more effective. The motivation is to have plenty of money left for you and for your family to enjoy what makes you happy.

We all have something to work on to achieve dreams and goals (unless we have achieved them all. If so, keep dreaming, as this is the spark of life; dreaming is free and entertaining). But what if you set out to achieve them?

You have your own dreams. Live them and never go after the dreams of others because we have all been created for different purposes. We are moved by different motives, and we have different experiences, fears, and weaknesses. If your idea is responsible and you have a good plan, but you feel afraid, keep moving ahead, even if that fear tries to paralyze you. Continue with the strength to take the first step. Overcoming fear is the key to confidence in yourself. Time will pass, and once you are there, in the place you wanted, you will realize that it was not as difficult as your self-mental-limits made you feel.

Don't be afraid of yourself or your family or friends. Remember that no one else can live your life, the life for which God created you, and that has a purpose that perhaps few understand but that you are passionate about, as if you have a baby that motivates you to keep going. When you want to beat that fear, pray, focus on your mission, and continue without looking back.

When we want to fix our car, we go and look at the manual from the company. We read all the information and all the instructions, and then we go and fix it because we have prepared ourselves to do it. But when it comes to finances, many people avoid the topic, they do not prepare, in many homes, they do not read about this issue, and they do not ask or respond to each other as a family on how to best manage it. In many cases, we are not even able to tell our financial problems to anyone, much less to a professional in the area, but God does know, so He left us a good tool so that right now you can prepare and start managing your money according to His principles and His holy will. It is a very good tool for your progress, so I recommend that you use it because, with this guide, you will achieve success.

> *"By wisdom a house is built, and through understanding it is established; through knowledge its rooms are filled with rare and beautiful treasures."*
> **— Proverbs 24:3-4, NIVUK**

Wisdom is not knowing or possessing certain information. It is information, knowledge, and understanding added to the criteria of knowing what is right. The Bible, in the book of James, chapter 1, teaches us that if we need wisdom, we can ask the Lord.

That said, I want to give you three practical tips and three principles of wisdom that will help you better manage your finances.

1. Pray regularly and start today. Start by asking for financial wisdom. He will grant it to you because He created you, and it is in your heart. He knows your intentions and why you do what you do. Start this today, do it! Prayer gives hope and life, and there does not have to be a fixed time set; it is like a constant conversation. Do it during meals, before bed, at work, or wherever you want, but start doing it as soon as possible. If you don't know how, you can repeat something like this: "Lord, I need your wisdom to manage my financial life and my business. I promise you that I will work with purpose, with my faith in you. Protect my home, my family, and my business. Amen." Don't underestimate the power of prayer.

2. Prudence is essential for long-term economic success. Many of the economic losses that we see in businesspeople around the world are due to misunderstandings, bad comments, rumors that were never verified, hasty investments, or imprudent decisions that did not allow them to put together a plan prudently. Being prudent is very important to keep you willing to continue your business in good and bad times until you succeed. Enjoy what you do, find your passion, plan wisely, use prudent words, be prudent in your relationships, be cautious with what you listen to, and apply prudence in your financial decision-making. Take a reasonable time to pray and seek guidance in

the word of God, both for small and large investments, since any step is very important in a business. Even though you feel that the Lord wants you to do something, be cautious because that may come from an emotion of the heart and not be from Him. If you have doubts, follow the Word of God.

3. Invest time in yourself, in learning, in filling your spirit. This is the strength you need to get ahead amid problems, and it is what will help you fall and get up faster and with a positive attitude. Set aside time to learn about how God wants you to manage the famous three Ts: time, talent, and treasures. This way, you will enjoy your finances and your processes.

Reflect:

*   Write down your dreams (minimum three; maximum ten).

---

*   Write down your debts, from smallest to largest, including amount, interest percentage, and what you pay monthly for each one, and write the total at the end.

- What would you do if you had that money left over each month? What dream from the list above would you achieve?

- Do you think you will be able to work with perseverance and discipline to achieve your goals? Why?

Why do you think so many people find it works to pay off the debt with the highest interest first? This is because your money is being invested in paying high percentages instead of reducing a debt; therefore, these types of expenses must be finished faster so that you can save more money, not paying so much interest.

If all your cards or debts have the same interest rate, why do you think it works for many people to start with the debt from the smallest to the largest? This is because finishing the smaller one is easier, and if the debt started with a very high rate or principal, you probably have a high minimum payment, so by eliminating that debt that is easier to pay, you will have more money left over to finish the debt that It follows in order, from smallest to largest.

The Importance of Savings

Prepare to have no financial worries when you are no longer able to work. Living with hunger is very difficult, and food costs are high. Being cold is horrible, and roof costs are high, so preparation is essential. You need to start saving now. Save what you can comfortably, plan with your family what they can do with the savings, and dream together.

Reflections:

- What goals do you have?

_____

_____

- What are your dreams and those you have as a family?

_____

_____

- How are these dreams going to fulfill them or fulfill you?

_____

_____

"The wise man saves for the future, [a] but the foolish man spends whatever he gets."

— Proverbs 21:20, TLB

> "*Take a lesson from the ants, you lazy fellow. Learn from their ways and be wise! For though they have no king to make them work, yet they labor hard all summer, gathering food for the winter.*"
>
> **— Proverbs 6:6-8, TLB**

Like the ant, we should save for future needs. It helps us to be cautious and protect ourselves, knowing that in any situation, we will be fine. It doesn't matter how old we are or how good we are; it is to know and feel that we are going to be well, that we have the finances to solve a problem, and that we can work because we want to, not because we have to.

We don't know when we will have the energy to persevere, so as long as you're healthy, enjoy your talents and save for the future.

Reflect:

- When you get older and if you ever get sick, are you prepared financially to support yourself with all your needs?

- Or who will give you everything you need?

- If it is a human and not God, what if, at that moment, that person can't?

So, we must be prepared for good times and bad to be able to survive.

About the Budget

Budgeting is a wise and useful way to manage your pocketbook and your financial progress. Many understand that budgeting is a smart way to keep track of their money, but how many have a written budget as part of their personal or family finances? Not many.

Having a written budget is very important because it allows you to have clarity on a personal and family level, as well as with your partners.

Budgets are needed in large and small businesses. Those who progress and live by their annual budgets have a map to know where they are located, and if there are additional expenses, this helps prevent excesses and maintain control.

Budgets are requested by administrative managers, shareholders, banks that provide loans for businesses, and, in some cases, even the government to qualify certain types of programs. If you want to have a sensible financial perspective, you need to have a budget.

Be faithful to your budget because when everything is covered as planned, there is more peace because the needs are covered, and the time you spend on these worries can be used to enjoy life with family, friends, and work without the finances being a problem.

Being diligent has extreme advantages. It develops this character, and this will help you solve effectively, focus on the solution, take days of worry off your back, and help your mind focus on moving forward. But act with firm steps, make wise decisions, and do not rush. A bad decision can cause you to lose money, so if you have doubts, you can diligently seek professional help.

A budget is nothing more than a plan for saving and spending money. Includes the source of the money and how much to expect, as well as the expenses to be covered, the money that comes in and the money that goes out, prioritizing needs before pleasure, such as rent or mortgage, utilities, food, gasoline, and insurance, also considering occasional or unexpected expenses.

When budgeting, when our salary arrives, the family already knows how much of that salary needs to be set aside to pay the bills that come and how much there is for extras, such as going out to dinner or going to the movies, traveling, investing and multiplying the money. Everything is planned and covered without uncertainties or false expectations.

If your case is that you work, you complain about money all the time, and you do not consider yourself a spendthrift, you urgently need to develop a plan to know where your money goes since it often disappears in small amounts that add up quickly.

To manage your money and your budget, you need discipline. Discipline helps you fulfill dreams that require money and allows you to have more financial and emotional stability while fulfilling them.

The principle of a wise businessman who wisely manages his assets and those of a family or business is not always easy, but with correct habits, it is enjoyed and achieved. This will probably mean having to postpone some purchases or forget to make them, but this will be temporary to seek future abundance. The men and women who can manage their resources wisely and carefully will see that their family and business needs will be met successfully.

Some Considerations About Money

1. Work willingly to enjoy any gain, knowing that God is the one who prospers you. When you forget the origin of your material blessings, you are in serious trouble.

2. Material absence or abundance does not evidence your spiritual state. Nobody is worth more or less for

their money. This concept will allow you to interact with society in a more real way, understanding that we are all equal. This allows any company to progress more since it can become more prosperous by helping more types of people.

3. We are slaves of our material possessions (See Leviticus 25:23). The problems increase when we believe that material goods are ours. God is sovereign, and He is the provider and sustainer of all we have.

4. Finances are a means by which God allows us to grow as godly people and as proof of our trust in Him.

5. It is good to be prosperous, but you must be convinced that money cannot buy security, nor do material goods fill the spirit. It is filled as you use it.

Wisdom in Money Management

The way we manage our finances has a lot to say about who we are internally as people: the things we value, the principles we obey, and the thought process we follow to make decisions. We need to produce an inner change to achieve an external change. If you're not very happy with your financial results, it's time to change your plan.

Debt can destroy relationships and, in some cases, even cause suicide, so this topic is very important. Scarcity, in certain circumstances, causes problems. The medal goes to the lack of seeking solutions that cause separations, breakups, and divorces in cases where finances are not well managed.

The right or wrong way to use finances is a situation that encompasses both believers and non-believers. Having money does not mean being spiritual. It is important to enjoy prosperity healthily and to help others; the satisfaction of successful people is living with purpose. This prevents the loss of energy and spiritual strength, prevents excuses, ignores a real problem, and avoids having feelings of emptiness.

Proverbs remind us that the Lord is very interested in the way we earn our living. We understand that He gives us talents to do good and use our gifts. Here is some wise advice extracted from the book of Proverbs that gives us biblical instruction regarding acquiring and using money.

> *"The Lord demands fairness in every business deal. [a] He established this principle."*
>
> **— Proverbs 16:11, TLB**

> *"Do not abuse the poor just because they are poor, nor be unfair to them in court."*
>
> **— Proverbs 22:22, NIV**

"If you are not honest, your money will not help you. But if you are righteous, it will save you from death."

— **Proverbs 10:2, EASY**

"A wicked person gets riches that soon disappear. But someone who lives in a good way will surely receive good things."

— **Proverbs 11:18, EASY**

"Wealth that comes from telling lies disappears quickly and leads to death."

— **Proverbs 21:6, ERV**

"Lazy hands will make you poor; hard-working hands will make you rich."

— **Proverbs 10:4, ERV**

"If you love to sleep too much, you will become poor. Keep awake so that you have food on the table!"

— Proverbs 20:13, EASY

Remember: Even for your protection, guarding against receiving money from people who have acquired it dishonestly is vital. You don't want to be involved in something like that or accumulate reasons for not having peace when sleeping. Keep in mind that there are too many businesses you can do honestly to make money and have peace.

Are you supporting something that, in the end, won't help you enjoy the harvest? Remember: the key is to enjoy prosperity with freedom with a huge satisfaction that you did it the right way; the feeling is awesome, enjoy it, and serve as an example for others to get ahead. We should never do the wrong thing to gain some profit. There are things more important than material benefits, such as peace, tranquility, harmony, and emotional and family stability. We must never change those priorities. They will bring you happiness and pride and be an example for your generation because you don't want to leave problems for someone you love.

Reflect

- Do you think you manage your finances well, or should you delegate?

_____

_____

- Do you have debts?

_____

_____

- Do you have savings?

_____

_____

- Do you feel peace when you talk about your finances?

_____

_____

- How would you like to feel about your financial situation?

_____

_____

- What decisions do you think you need to make to help you to improve your finances?

_____

_____

The Door of Prosperity Awaits You

The key to your business is found in the sum of your potential and your purpose.

Throughout the book, we have accumulated tools that help us motivate ourselves to achieve our dreams and, most importantly, take action to achieve them and put diligence into the matter. It's not intensity; it's using that passion and purpose that you have to diligently do what needs to be done.

Because yes, it is good to have wealth, we must break down the paradigm that the rich are bad or that money is not good. It is important that at least you are clear about your interpretation so that these comments do not bring you negativity and change your positive mind, making you feel guilty for having prosperity as God wants you to have it. If you look carefully and read a little more about this, you will see that the abundance comes from God; the problem is not having money but loving it in a way that takes away your peace or affects someone with it.

> *"For the love of money is the root of all evil; and while some have coveted after it, they have erred from the faith and pierced themselves through with many sorrows."*
>
> **— 1 Timothy 6:10, KJ21**

The only love must be toward God to prevent problems. The faith should be in Him, in his purpose. If we humiliate someone with money, it is already a destructive weapon and not convenient for the one who handles it, and with that attitude, you lose family, friends, and people who could have been of prosperity.

Love for Jesus and obedience to his principles are the keys to success. When we work with love, as if we work for God, money and all its blessings will come. Don't suffer for money; suffer if you lose the quality of the work you do for God. That is different.

If your car is broken, don't suffer, just fix it. If you have to pay a bill, just pay it, don't even think about it. Or if you don't have the money, focus on the solution to get it and be able to pay for what is taking away your peace.

If you love money more than purpose, you need to change your way of thinking. If you don't, you will stop enjoying God's blessings.

Accepting that it is important to work on your finances, using your talents, not giving up on your dreams with faith, and asking God to give you wisdom is a big step. As I wrote before, you will see how He will guide you to the right people, open doors for you, help you sustain yourself, and give you the way so that you can help and empower the people you love to be financially successful. Ask God to teach you how to manage the money and your finances.

He works miracles, and He can change our minds if something negative does not work out. He lets us move on. He is capable of giving us abundance if he believes that we will use the money for good. He knows our hearts.

To be rich is to live life not for yourself but for God. It's living a life motivated by loving God with all the heart, soul, mind, and forces. I believe that when God sees this in your heart, He fills you with abundance because He knows that your soul belongs to Him and not to money.

After Jesus' conversation with a rich young man (Matthew 19:16–22), Jesus says something remarkable (v. 23): "Truly I say to you, it will be difficult for a rich man to enter the kingdom of heaven." He had just promised eternal life to a young man if he would sell all his possessions, give the money to the poor, and follow him. That challenge was intended only for that man, not for all people, because this young man demonstrated that he was not truly willing to obey God. The man could not or would not do it.

This doesn't mean that Jesus thought money was bad; it just showed that the rich young man loved money more than he loved Jesus. So, if Jesus proposed sharing wealth with the poor, it is because Jesus wanted wealth for the poor. He loved the poor and the rich.

This showed that it is okay to receive financial blessings from God if you help others with it. The proof is that God also loves the poor, and that is why he wanted to share this money with them; therefore, he did not consider money bad.

"If you try to get money quickly, you will not stay rich for long. But if you are patient, you will become rich little by little."

— Proverbs 13:11, EASY

Part Five:
The Master Key

Entrepreneur's Guide

———————————

B elow, you will find a guide that will summarize all the meanings of the keys you need to open the door to success in your business. Start now as a winner!

Five Tips For You

1. **Learn to say no:** If what they propose to you or what you want is not in your budget, If doing so harms your company or your employees, or if it compromises your values, your health, or your well-being, the answer should always be no!

2. **Educate yourself:** Nothing will help you grow more than education. Look for all the courses, workshops, seminars, or training you need to grow in what your business needs, including your financial wisdom.

Proverbs 4:7, ERV

"The first step to becoming wise is to look for wisdom, so use everything you have to get understanding."

---

3. **Seek advice:** Seek advice from professionals, an experienced family member, a successful businessperson, or even a debt counselor. The experts can help you establish a budget and manage your income, expenses, and debts, as this can put you on the path to taking care of your family in the best way possible. Listen to those with more experience, those who cross your path, and especially investors. Humility is basic in learning. Whether you like it or not, you must develop learning from others. It can cost you much more to learn the hard way by yourself. Listening to advice and suggestions does not mean that you have to do everything they tell you, but you will be able to make your own decisions with a broader perspective after listening and analyzing with the right intention to grow.

4. **Have a good circle of support:** You are going to invest a lot of time, resources, and energy in your new business adventure, so you will need people close to you who love and support you, starting with your

immediate circle, that is, your family. Talk to them, explain that this process will challenge them financially and emotionally, and try to get them to agree. Keep in mind that it is normal for them to be nervous at first and not be able to fully show you their support, especially if they do not know the field you want to venture into and do not have the same mentality as you, but instead of getting frustrated, respect their opinion and show them with facts who you are. If no one supports you, remember that this is your dream and your struggle. The process will be easier if you have them, but motivation is your responsibility, not theirs, and there are other groups and business circles that you can rely on and drive you to grow. Of course, even if you don't have the support of your family when something good happens to you, celebrate with them so that the people who love you see your prosperity. Use your family as motivation to move forward and lead a better life.

5. **Have Faith**: Faith in business has been essential for me, and it is advice that I give you regardless of your religion. Believe, do not doubt, and move forward. Believe in God, or your higher power, and believe in yourself.

What You Can't-Miss

1. Legal structure

Consult with your accountant or a professional in the area where you live on what is best for you: being a sole proprietor, having a partner, being part of a cooperative, forming a limited liability company, a corporation, or having a non-profit organization. Remember that each place in the world has its laws and regulations.

Define it and write it here:

My legal structure is _____

2. A name

Decide on a name that goes with your business idea that will be your brand. Then, check if the name you chose is available for the legal registrations of businesses in your area and also in internet domains. This is very important to avoid customer confusion and also to determine if you can use it freely in your country and state.

Define it and write it here:

The name of my company is _____

3. Your company registration

If the name you want is available, you feel comfortable, it is what you want, and it matches your ideal, register it as soon as possible in the corresponding offices. If it is impossible for you, the patent can wait. Patents can cost a lot of money, and registering your ideas is more affordable. Many entrepreneurs recommend paying this amount only if the product demands a patent and when you are sure that you will get enough customers to settle the accounts.

Check this **box** if you already have:

☐ I have a registered company, or I require a patent.

4. A marketing plan

Take advantage of free resources such as social networks, but if you have the opportunity, working with an expert who offers you advice and experience to move your project forward will be very advantageous.

Check this **box** if you already did:

☐ I managed to define my marketing plan and/or contact an expert for it.

5. Protection and security

Make sure you have the right insurance to protect your company and you as a business owner, especially against lawsuits. This will help you work more calmly since you will be protected in case of an error.

Insurance can vary depending on the type of business and the area in which you live. If you work from home or at a location, make sure your insurance also includes theft of equipment and documentation, as well as liability for damages related to the same.

Check this **box** if you already have:

☐   I have already taken out all the insurance
I need, and my company is protected.

---

6. Clean accounts

Keep accounting books up to date, with clarity and extreme organization. Many companies sell a lot and do very well but are ultimately forced to close due to poor management. Make it a non-negotiable rule not to spend more than you earn; Learn to grow with profits, not debt. Organization in a company is vital. It records absolutely all the money that enters and leaves the business. If you don't like paperwork and numbers or don't feel capable, hire someone who is, but keep in mind that a business without good management simply doesn't work. A big problem for those who want to start a business is that they dream of having everything and starting big, and seeing it so difficult due to the debts that this entails, they don't start and prefer to do nothing. But from experience, I can tell you that it's okay to start small, and it's even more satisfying when you see progress.

In my case, for example, to start one of the last businesses I started in 2008, I did not have enough resources. It was a service-based business, and I started by subleasing a small office with just two well-fitted desks. As I told you in previous chapters, over time, I was able to move to a larger office and then to another larger one, using only the profits of the same company to grow little by little. Sometime later, many doors opened to me, and I was blessed to have my agency in a very good location, right next to a main avenue in Winter Park, Florida. I rented there for approximately ten years before buying a place where I had the opportunity to now be the one who could sublease spaces to others as the owner of other offices.

If I had not started from the bottom humbly, if I had spent without order to have everything big from the beginning, if I had mismanaged the resources that came in, this would not have happened, and it would not even have started.

7.   A suitable location

If your type of business allows you to work at home or remotely, a good formula to reduce expenses is to do it from home. But you should also keep in mind that many clients like to have a place to go and see that the business exists, which gives them greater credibility about the stability of the company. To do this, some companies offer the double option of working remotely and also have a place to present to clients. However, times have been changing especially after the COVID-19 pandemic and people now see it as more common and acceptable for people to telework.

I recommend that you analyze the following factors:

- What presence is good for your business?

- Do you want to expand, or is your ideal a business where you can or need to be with your family at home?

- Analyze where you can focus more.

- Are there unprofessional noises in your chosen work environment that a customer will hear when they call?

This is very important because, believe it or not, what customers hear in the background of a call can lead to a sale or, on the contrary, retain them with an image of professionalism. What they receive on the other end of the line, especially if they don't know you physically, can convey a lot or a little credibility for your business. Remember that the client must feel that they are calling a serious and stable company, and they need to listen clearly to what you explain. Don't lower your quality levels. Choose a location that suits the needs of your business, that offers you an opportunity to grow, proper accessibility for customers, and the appropriate level of competition and proximity for suppliers. Now, keep in mind that if it is not necessary, you should not worry about an office; **you should Make it a Reality Now.** If you cannot have your own space to work, you can do it from home or from a place where you are comfortable, according to your income, where you enjoy your process, have peace, and where your business gets to be successful.

Your "always yes, yes, yes"

- **Should I post on my social media all the time? Yeah!**

   The business must stay alive, and social networks are an ideal space to reflect to your current and potential clients that you are active. Don't feel bad about sharing your triumphs, desires, and struggles; seek to motivate and help with your products. Clients will enjoy your honesty and delivery with each new piece of information.

- **Should I create and offer new products and services regularly? Yeah!**

   Your customers must know the variety of products you have. Make promotional packages and make sure you take care of them by giving them new products or services. If your business allows it, buy large quantities of products because the more products you buy, the more discounts you will get, and you will have a greater profit margin.

Don't stay with stagnant products. Many companies fail because they do not take the action of getting rid of products in which they invested a lot of money, maintaining a product without rotation and with expenses that do not suit anyone. If you've already tried doing the right marketing, and it still doesn't work, reinvent yourself.

- **Should I be patient and stay focused? Of course!**

  Wait and focus on what you have to do, always keeping in mind that success does not come overnight. Don't get frustrated right away. Many people think that because you are not a millionaire, you are not successful, but are you happy with what you do? Does it give you health? Does it give you joy? Does what you do allow you to be happy with the people you care about? Your company is not a failure if you are not a millionaire. On the contrary, it is admirable that you have the great courage to have and live from your business. If you receive profits generated by doing something you are passionate about, it is already a great success story; do not despair. But also stay positive because you can become a millionaire if you follow the process. If possible. This dream can also come true, it is proven.

This may take some time before you earn anything. Some businesses take months, and others take years since, depending on the type of business, usually, the first months are spent recovering what was invested. For that reason, it is good to have reserves to be calmer and enjoy the process.

- **Should I maintain good relationships with clients, employees, and partners, seeking the best for everyone? Yeah! That will make you different.**

Harmony is essential in business since many details must be resolved every day, and the idea is to enjoy the process with peace. Once you have a new client, you must not only ensure that they are satisfied with your products and services, but you must go further, providing a solution to their problems. Pay attention specifically to their needs; that way, you will have a high probability of having this customer for life. But if your idea is initially rejected by customers, investors, or others, don't take it personally or entertain your anger. Be grateful for what you receive only to be better and allow honesty in people. Find out what they didn't like, listen, make adjustments, and come back to them once you've changed what they wanted. This is a quick way to grow.

If you have problems with an employee, make sure they are resolved. Apologize if you treat them badly. If you make a mistake, look for solutions without blaming someone for something you did. Injustice doesn't work for anyone; the feelings stay, and that affects your business. Don't talk behind anyone's back. Look for polite words of respect because we are all equal, we are all looking for a common goal, and we all deserve to progress. With Discord, it is difficult to get a project out.

If you have a problem, try to solve it as soon as possible, even if you don't always "win." Sometimes, what seems like a loss turns into a gain because your mood and motivation are worth much more. Don't let time pass because the more time passes, the more opportunities you will give for misinterpretations. Fights and misunderstandings can be big distractions that take away your focus from doing things right in your business.

- **Should I bring more people to my business? Yes, but analyzing your decisions is very good!**

Is it a lot of work that consumes your time? Seek help, extend hours, change prices, and improve your service. You must learn to delegate, form teams, and determine if it is a good option for your business. You must also carefully analyze the pros and cons when partnering. If you do not delegate, this will consume your time since it is impossible for you to cover all positions without making mistakes.

If, at some point, a partner acquires a share of your company, you must recognize the fact that you will eventually have to give up some control of the business. From then on, every time a decision has to be made, it will not be yours alone. And if the shared part is greater than 50%, that part will have more votes (if they established it so). Be careful of your decisions and how much you give when you join.

Chapter Summary:

The Twenty Essentials

1. You can write professional emails and template letters for your clients.

Correct communication with your clients is crucial because something poorly written or open to misinterpretation can cost you everything from your professional image to legal repercussions. From the beginning, define the communications you approved to send to your clients so you will always know exactly what your employees are sending. This way, you protect the company and your relationships with clients. If you don't feel ready to compose these highly professionally written communications, hire someone who knows how to do it, preferably a person or agency related to communications, marketing, or public relations. This person will also be able to help you with press releases and other official communications that will publicize company news.

2. Prepare your material for your training.

In Chapter 14, we talked about it. Read it again if you feel like you need to remember it.

3. Make a plan for your team before each meeting.

Every time you meet with your team, define in advance the topics you want to cover and send them this plan so that they can prepare and give you their opinion to improve the deficiencies and reinforce everything positive. This will help you make good decisions. Your team's opinion is very important, so you need to make sure everyone understands these topics clearly.

4. Hire suitable employees.

A company is formed with a strong team, and we all have different talents. Hire people with skills in the areas you need most to combine talents and cover all needs. When people are in the right place, and everyone does what they like, they are more loyal, and you enjoy the process more.

Don't give up or settle with anyone who doesn't take care of your business; treat them like a son to whom you don't want anything to happen, and you want to put them in the right hands.

5. **Benefit from referrals and what people say about your business.**

Good marketing is getting your business from word of mouth. Look for people who influence others, and let your friends, family, and influencers spread the word about what your company, your products, or your services do. That's why it is important to maintain good relationships to help move your company forward and obtain referrals from your clients and their positive comments.

6. **Organize and attend formal and informal social and entertainment events.**

Don't be afraid to share with others or go out to show your product and your face to the public at community events, conferences, and meetings, but also when you go to the supermarket, go out with a friend, and enjoy the networking. Talk about your product all the time and create good relationships with people inside and outside your sector because you never know where you might find a great opportunity.

7. **Conquer all the senses of your clients.**

It is important that you create your business cards and flyers—physical and digital—where you communicate what you are and what you offer and that you distribute everything wherever you can, but it is also important that you take into account sensory marketing to make it more effective. This means that you know what the correct elements are for the image of your product or brand (colors, fonts, icons, among others), but also, if you have an event or a physical space, you determine what lights, temperature, music, and even aromas are ideal for transmitting sensations and conquering the senses of your consumers.

8. Provide customer service that exceeds any expectations.

Be proud of what you give, and enjoy the feeling that your business goes much further than making money. Enjoy your processes with the people who are important to your work. Your business could gain new customers if you make them feel valuable. Master your customer service, analyze what words, tone of voice, and attitude are being used to serve them, and do it better and better. This way you will gain many buyers and your profits will increase.

Don't settle for comfort; find people who listen and are good at following instructions and paying attention to detail. One of the keys to customer service is listening, and if someone does it well, your customers will feel that they do not have to insist too much to have something simple resolved, and that is reflected in sales. On the contrary, if a team member always wants to be right and do the opposite of what a client wants, they will be filled with frustration and feel like they are wasting their time, and of course, that will also be seen in your sales.

In the face of bad service, it is your company that looks bad and loses customers. That is why you should hire ideal people for each position and observe their natural talents, their attitudes, and their learning capacity. Even if it is your business, you won't always be able to deal with everything, which is why you need qualified people to complete the job.

Be quick in your deliveries. There is nothing worse than hiring the services of someone who does not keep their promises. Set real times, even if this is a little more than you need. It is better to look like a hero by delivering work faster than promised than to look bad later for not being able to deliver. Failure to comply is a reflection of bad business. You are there to help the consumer, not to create anxiety and stress in the process. Communicate with the customer, explain what is happening and why, and enjoy pleasing them. Remember that the objective is not to leave that client but to fulfill them with excellence to maintain your reputation and your good reviews and also receive referrals. Business is a work in progress, and if you promote a product or service with fast delivery, you will be able to build a community of customers who will provide you with valuable opinions that will help you improve your quality.

9. Make sure you have a working website.

Customers who enter and view information should have options to purchase your product or contact you to hire your services. Potential customers want to have as much information as possible about your business, and if they can get all the answers there, it will be the most practical for you and them. Strive for quick and complete access since if it is easy to navigate, sales will increase.

10. Don't be afraid to compete with a more experienced business.

The world evolves with new technologies and innovative ideas. If you are creative, enjoy doing different things. Never speak badly of the competition or try to generate pity because that only affects you. If they offer a product or service that you don't, don't speculate about them.

When you are with clients or investors, do not put anyone down to raise yourself because this makes you look unprofessional. Also, remember that if you talk about them, positively or negatively, you are indirectly giving them publicity, and perhaps this will have the opposite effect and make customers go to the competition.

11. Don't worry so much about your finances; worry about doing well and not giving up. Some of the best businesses were launched when the economic situation was not the best for the world. I, in particular, started one of the businesses at a time when the economy was very bad, and there were people losing homes and businesses. Whenever I mentioned that I wanted to start a business, a lot of people told me that it was not the time. Now, many years later, the company is increasingly in its best moments. So don't think about it so much and go for it!

12. Pray for your business and be honest.

To progress, you have to let go, you have to trust, and you have to pray. Trust that when you have a good purpose with your company, your higher force will take care of your things and protect your business. In my case, as I told you before, my highest strength is God. Honesty is essential. When you can, you can, and when you can't, you can't. Don't commit to something you're not sure you can do.

13. Have a balance between social life, business, and family.

Dedicate time to each of the important areas of your life and respect those times so that you give your one hundred percent to them. Don't mix. When it's time to work, it's time to work, so don't be distracted by interruptions. Focus. At first, it will take more time because the foundation must be firm and stable before resting. If it's time with family or friends, share, give your attention to your loved ones, and make them feel important. It's their time. In the end, why do we work so hard if not to have and enjoy the life we want with the people we love and who love us?

Also, dedicate time to yourself, think about what makes you happy, and give yourself time to work on your happiness, your well-being, and your moments of purpose. Manage your time and respect them to achieve your goals. Excesses in everything are bad and destroy you. Enjoy your time and your responsibilities intelligently.

14. Accept when it's time to leave.

Are you getting into debt and can't take it anymore? So, this is not a business; it is already causing damage, and maybe it is time to reinvent yourself. Something like this is not easy to accept, but it works with your ego, with your pride, with what others will say. What matters is you and your life. If you've tried everything and failure is inevitable, that's okay. It's brave to try. Put your pride aside, and if there is no solution to maintain it, don't sink, just close. Think about what is convenient for you and how your business is affecting you, and make the decision. If it is for the best, you have to do it. Some people are better suited to work for someone, and that's fine too. Without people like that, we wouldn't be able to sustain companies either because it is thanks to the workers that many companies move forward. Make your decision in time, and remember that you have not lost anything by trying. Before making this decision, make sure you try everything first.

15. Listen to advice, but also trust yourself.

Ask friends and family for feedback on your ideas. Remember that the people closest to you may be your next clients, and if they are not, they are human beings who consume and are the ones who will be most honest with you about your idea. Ask a lot of questions and understand the reason for their answers. Don't hesitate to seek their advice and suggestions constructively, but while I am also giving you advice, something I learned the hard way is that although many people offer their help, you are the owner of the business and the one responsible for its success or failure. If you know what works, you will have the skills and knowledge to move your business forward. You are not the experiences or talents of others; you are unique.

16. Stay away from negative people and ignore those you can't avoid.

There is a huge difference between constructive criticism made for your growth and the words of someone who quickly tells you that your business will fail just because of their negativity. The best thing you can do is analyze what makes sense and what doesn't about what people tell you and see if they are giving you their opinion from a place of fear and failure or one of honesty and experience. Much of what they tell you comes from the personality of the commenter and is not related to your personality, dreams, product, or your faith.

17. Be flexible. As time progresses and experiences grow, the chances increase that your original idea will have to be modified. Being able to adapt and change something convenient to offer the customer something they want will determine whether or not you will succeed positively. It is your responsibility to find what works, leave it, and discard what harms your business.

18. Make sure your clients pay the bills.

Make sure you receive payment for your product or service with fair and adequate prices. Don't let them take advantage of you, so set a time for payments to be made. If you have the option, consider accepting credit cards or having the option for them to pay directly on your website.

19. Be careful with credit cards.

It is very common, especially with credit cards, not to analyze what interest rate they are giving. You have to be very careful because these expenses can consume your profits. Staying with the first offer is not a good option. You should look for the best and only accept it if it makes sense and if you can easily cover that debt with the profits of the product you offer. If you necessarily have to get a card, analyze your personal needs carefully. See if it has an annual cost or if you are benefiting from having it. Do not use a credit card if you want luxuries; only use it for extreme needs or emergencies. If you have money left over after paying your responsibilities, don't spend what you don't have. Covering needs first is a decision made by wise people and good home administrators. Sometimes, the decision is easy, but whims do not allow you to see how these decisions can affect your stability and peace.

20. Enjoy!

Celebrate each achievement, try to surround yourself with people who make you happy, who have the same values as you, and who feel happy for you. Enjoy your processes, and do healthy, crazy things. And why not if life is short?

"The LORD will always lead you and satisfy your needs in dry lands. He will give strength to your bones. You will be like a garden that has plenty of water, like a spring that never goes dry."

— Isaiah 58:11, ERV

Epilogue:

How can you overcome obstacles to make your business successful in a meaningful and fulfilling way?

As I told you at the beginning, since I was little, I saw so much poverty and so many homeless people—children and adults—on the streets. As I was just a girl, in the middle of my innocence, I did not understand that there were so many reasons why a person could be in situations like this or with problems such as drug use and so many mental, emotional, and physical illnesses. When I saw people suffering from hunger, cold, and so many other situations, this caused me inner pain, but the thought of that being my future paralyzed me. This made my mind creative, and I was looking for opportunities for it.

Without fully understanding what was happening, as a child, I entertained myself by watching advertisements for different businesses on the streets, and I did not understand how, with so many possibilities of creating something exciting, someone preferred to be bored and uncomfortable, exposing themself to so many things that can happen to someone for not being able to provide for a safe roof. Obviously, at that time, I did not understand the responsibility, conditions, and effort that all this required, but I think that seeing so much need when I was little awakened something in me, and it reflected later in my life. But from a very young age, my head kept creating constant ideas for its use. Instead of doing nothing and suffering from needs, I suffered a lot from seeing people like that, but I really couldn't do anything, not only because of my age but because I had no control. I only dreamed for the sake of dreaming. The sensitivity I had at that time as a weakness is my greatest strength today.

When I was in high school, helping create sources to raise funds for our classmate's plans was extremely fun because sometimes we prepared food together to sell to other students. For example, for our graduation trip, I loved to encourage my classmates to do activities or whatever we could think of to get funds. I even ran as a candidate for president of the school without any shame of going from room to room, presenting my candidacy in a fun way. It was around seventh grade, and when I was finishing my last year of school, I made my first "big" business. I laugh just remembering that experience!

At that time, Spanish rock parties were in fashion, which we called "Los zafarranchos," so together with two other wonderful friends, We rented a place in an old building, which was still brick, to organize our party. We made flyers with a lot of advertising, we bought the necessary drinks and things to sell, and we got lights, music, and equipment. We even invented activities like "the hydro-jet," which was hanging hoses with very small holes that would throw water around the building in the middle of the night, which, since the building was made of concrete, did not cause damage. The idea was great; people were so happy that we filled the place, and with the results, we raised enough money with which we were able to pay off everything, including our music equipment, lights and had a lot of savings for the next event, which was something very difficult to get since we were very young.

Sometime later, my father took over a place like a minimarket, a small store, which my sisters and I ran. I didn't last long there because our tastes, opinions, and ideas were very different, so I decided to go to work in a clothing store and a restaurant where my opinions were heard. I liked my job, and in my free time, I helped in the store with my sisters until my family decided it was time to move to the United States.

We arrived in 1998 without knowing any English. We started working in a fast-food place and studying the language. I left every day at that first job in my new country with my face full of grease, hot from the grills or wet from washing dishes, but happy to have a job.

After that, I had other jobs, but there was always that passion for business in my heart. For me, it was fun and too exciting to search for and promote crazy and healthy ideas. I was very happy when someone wanted to start a business, and I loved to see that out of nothingness and fear, they found courage, passion, and risk, and they began to do much better than when they had their previous job.

My first entrepreneurial experience in the United States was in a small natural products store, but after this, I made the decision not to have businesses where I had to buy products to sell because the investment was high and the risk was higher. So, I decided to look for a service business, and I managed to sell the business I had built, recovering everything invested plus profits.

That's how I decided to get my license to work in real estate. I wanted to work with people, and my dream was to have multiple properties, fully paid, with no mortgage, and retire with the income. At that moment, I did not know that God would multiply in abundance everything that I had once lost and that my dream would also multiply as an investor. Due to many personal circumstances, I moved to Miami, where I had to start another career, this time in the insurance business.

During the six months of being in Miami, I got a job where I was doing very well, but before starting, I told the owner that I would only work with him for a specific time, but that, in exchange for the experience I would gain, I told him that I promised to increase sales figures and I achieved it. Even without experience, I set a goal and achieved it using all the methods reflected in this book.

However, on a personal level, things were not going as well as business, and after much pain, I decided to return to Orlando to spend as much time as possible with my mother, who was dying of cancer. That same month, she died in my arms. I watched as her organs shut down one by one until, finally, her soul was gone. For me, it was a gift to be able to have her and hold her in that moment. I was alone. Many people waited for the last moment to come to be with her, but God allowed me to be there in her last breath. It was a death that separated us physically, but it allowed me to tell her how much I loved her and how grateful I was for raising me. It was a very difficult moment, but I knew that she was not going to suffer anymore with so much pain, and when I felt sad and missed her a lot, my solution was to imagine her full of peace, love, fullness, and joy, with the best feelings next to God, and that gave me peace.

After her death, I was again starting from scratch, without a job because I moved to Orlando again, and full of pain, with a commitment made to a previous company, which I had to fulfill. So I started again at the same company but in Orlando instead of Miami. I doubled my sales production as I had promised. Not only had I lost my mother, but I had also gone through a divorce in which I lost my marriage, my other family, many who claimed to be my friends, and all the assets I had acquired so far. I felt alone, walking with the world on top of me. At that moment, I only had God, who did not let me fall, who presented me with the right people to help me. At the same time, that loneliness helped me in a very positive way to start working on my business.

After a year of my work commitment, I resigned, and I started everything to open my own office. In deep sadness, I found a way to distract my mind and focus on work while overcoming more obstacles than I ever imagined I would have to face.

But also, in that moment of brokenness, I was going through one of the best decisions I could make, which was to open my own business, and I want to tell you something wonderful that happened years after when I least expected it:

When I was donating my time to a Christian news program providing financial advice to help the community, a guest pastor arrived and said, "I have a prophecy for you: 'Don't worry, my daughter, that everything will happen again. Everything you lost once, God is saying: I am going to multiply in abundance what you lost, and you will cross borders to teach about me." And in fruits, it multiplied ten times and more like one of the stories told previously. God always looked for a way to lift me and make me feel like I wasn't alone. How can I not love God intensely? How can I not get on my knees and want to work for Him? How can I not ask Him to enlighten me and use me to help others?

Thanks to saving money for the future and receiving financial blessings from God, I was able to open my own business in 2008, which is still ongoing. The office was able to bless others with good salaries that helped their families be better off.

To this day, God has given me much more than what I lost, not only financially but also with a beautiful family made with a man full of love for me and a beloved and wonderful son that I did not have before. God changed me, multiplied all the friendships I lost, and healed my heart. That is the love that I feel, filled with a lot of gratitude.

I feel that to help you with your finances, I have to help you realize that money, prosperity, and good things come from God. If you think that money comes from evil, you will feel guilty, and the only one affected will be you, not me, because I am convinced that money and abundance come from Him. I know it not from words and imagination but from fruits and real events that I have experienced. These tips expressed in this book have been working with my family, with my businesses, and with the businesses of my friends who followed this path, and it can work for you, too, if you receive in abundance and acceptance of everything God has for you.

Yes, you can move forward and start from scratch if necessary. I hope you have enjoyed this work that was made with all my heart for you and with the intention that all these experiences can serve you in the future. I hope that your life is filled with much prosperity, love, and well-being, and may you know that if you have God in your heart, you will always be well. Whatever bad happens to you will be for your good.

Don't lose faith. Stay there, and do whatever you have to do to overcome life's obstacles. If you act in good faith, you will be fine. Always remember that life is temporary, and we have a purpose. Make your life count, and understand that you were created for something important, and that's why you go through what you do and you have what you have.

Please take good care of yourself, and if you think it can help someone, share my experience. I saw God's financial blessing, and you can see it too. Continue forward with your dream, surround yourself with the right people, follow all the advice I have given you in this book, and make a decision that will change your life. Don't do it tomorrow; don't wait for another sign. This is the time. Make It a Reality... NOW!

Acknowledgments

I feel grateful because I know that the tears, the joys, and all the blessings that God gave me with so much love will not be in vain and because through this book, many lives will be touched that need help to move forward and receive prosperity.

I am grateful for my parents, who are not here with me anymore, but thanks to them, I am who I am now. To my grandmother, who taught me about God at every opportunity, I would not be here now if I did not feel God was always with me.

I especially thank my beloved José Rodríguez, who has so patiently supported me in my adventures, and my son Diego Rodríguez, who was my motivation to leave a legacy with this book as a guide of love for him and anyone I care about. From my heart, I hope this book may help a lot of people.

I thank the readers because this book would not have validity without them. Thank you to all those who supported me in this challenge, those who motivated me, and those who continue to support me.

Thanks to all the entrepreneurs who shared their stories. But, above all, I want to thank and dedicate this book to God for never abandoning me and because I am his creation.

About the Author

L eidis Bedoya was born in Medellín, Colombia, and in 1998, she traveled to live permanently in Florida. She is the second of three sisters and the fruit of parents who left their persistence, encouragement, positivism, and dedication as an example. She currently lives with her family in Lake Mary, FL. They are her greatest motivation to get ahead.

Leidis has more than twenty years of experience as a businesswoman. She is CEO of Florida Protective Insurance, Fl Protective Investments, and Haz que Pase Ya, LLC., among other companies. She started her first business at the age of sixteen, and after more business experience helping many start their ventures and working with the community, she ended her degree, a specialization in business, and her international certification in business coaching at UCF, adding a touch of mastery to the strategies and advice she shares in this book. She is not only a professional with an impressive skill set but also a passionate community member dedicated to altruistic missions.

As a thank you for so many blessings, Leidis enjoys getting involved in community help projects, which is why she is cofounder of the *Love for Africa event*. She has participated in projects such as *Real Life Projects*, *Feed the Homeless*, *Missionaries of the Poor*, and *Traveling to Africa on the Mission*. She also has a YouTube channel where she provides advice to help the community. She is a creator, business coach, and producer in social work.

Leidis has not only created *"Make It a Reality Now"* to provide you with practical tools for business success but also to inspire you through lessons based on faith and hope. Leidis Bedoya invites you on a fun and transformative journey to overcome obstacles, grow your business, and live the life you always dreamed of. Don't miss the opportunity to take advantage of her teachings and transform your business and life today!

Contact Information

Author: Leidis Bedoya

www.hazquepaseya.com

Haz que pase ya LLC

2500 W Lake Mary Blvd Suite 107

Lake Mary, Fl., 32746

The Back Cover

MAKE IT A REALITY NOW!

> *"How you can overcome obstacles to make your business successful in a meaningful and fulfilling way."*

This book is not just a business guide; it is a beacon of Christian MOTIVATION designed to ignite your dreams and take you to new heights in your entrepreneurship.

From her roles as an investor and Professional Certified in Real Estate and Insurance to CEO of multiple companies, the author of this book shares her valuable knowledge to help you start, continue, and live fully through your business. Her more than two decades of business experience support every page of this book.

Through an immersive narrative, Leidis transfers her successful SECRETS to be adapted to SUCCEED anywhere in the world. Her degree and specialization in business and her International Certification in Business Coaching add a touch of mastery to the STRATEGIES and tips she shares.

The author is not only a professional with an impressive set of skills but also a passionate member of the community, dedicated to altruistic missions.

"Make It a Reality Now" will not only provide you with practical tools for business success but inspire you through lessons based on faith and hope.

Leidis Bedoya invites you on a fun trip and transformative journey to overcome obstacles, grow your business, and live the life you always dreamed of.

Don't miss the opportunity to take advantage of her teachings and transform your business and your life NOW!

ENJOY YOUR LIFE, REAP THE FRUITS OF YOUR BUSINESS, and MAKE IT A REALITY NOW!

Available at www.hazquepaseya.com

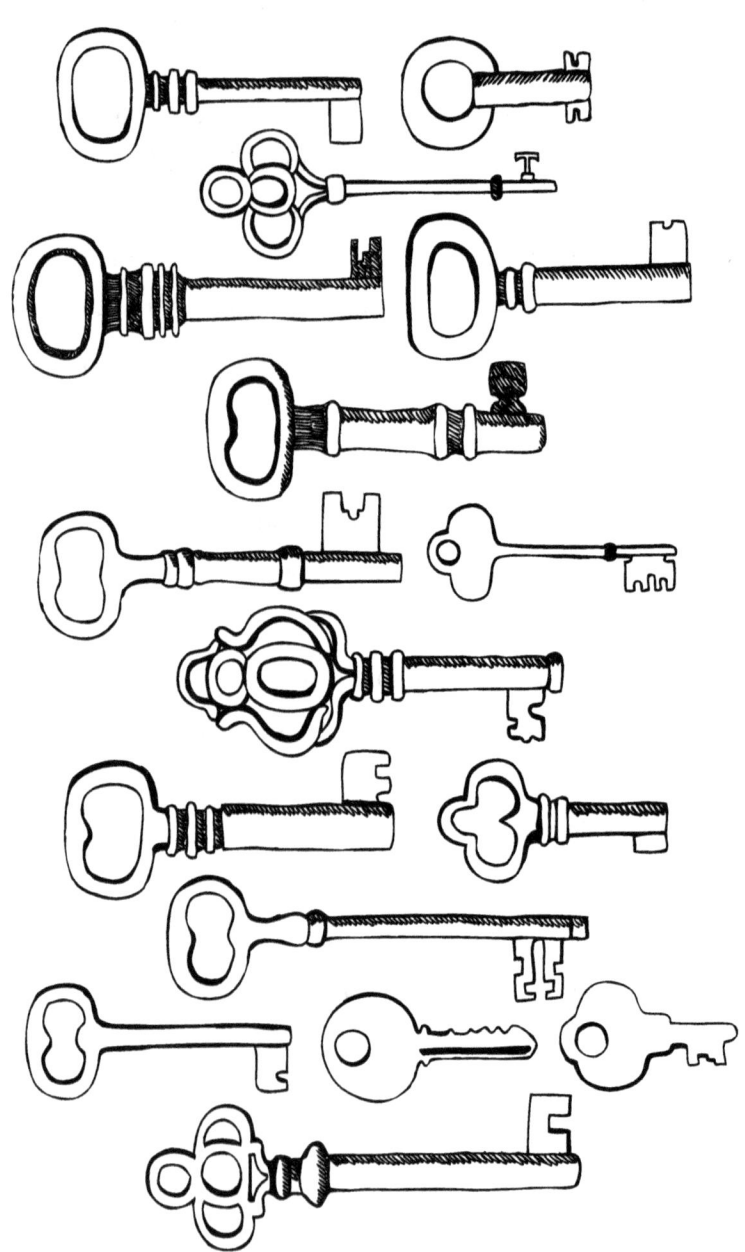

Notes

Notes